|||| | ||| |||||| || | || ||||||| |||||||||| | || |||
☟ **W9-AXE-199**

Unbelievably Good Deals
& Great Adventures
That You
Absolutely Can't Get
Unless You're Over

50

Unbelievably Good Deals
& Great Adventures
That You
Absolutely Can't Get
Unless You're Over
50

JOAN RATTNER HEILMAN

CB

CONTEMPORARY
BOOKS

A TRIBUNE NEW MEDIA COMPANY

Library of Congress Cataloging-in-Publication Data

Heilman, Joan Rattner.
    Unbelievably good deals & great adventures that you absolutely
can't get unless you're over 50 / Joan Rattner Heilman. — 7th
updated ed.
        p.   cm.
    Includes index.
    ISBN 0-8092-3426-2 (paper)
    1. Travel.   2. Discounts for the aged.   I. Title.   II. Title:
Unbelievably good deals and great adventures that you absolutely
can't get unless you're over 50.
G151.H44   1995
910.4—dc20   95-3404
                                                                  CIP

Cover design by Georgene Sainati
Cover and interior illustrations by Denise Harnish

Copyright © 1995, 1994, 1993, 1992, 1990, 1989, 1988 by Joan Rattner
Heilman
All rights reserved
Published by Contemporary Books, Inc.
Two Prudential Plaza, Chicago, Illinois 60601-6790
Manufactured in the United States of America
Library of Congress Catalog Card Number: 88-377
International Standard Book Number: 0-8092-3426-2

Contents

Chapter One
Introduction to Good Deals and Great Adventures

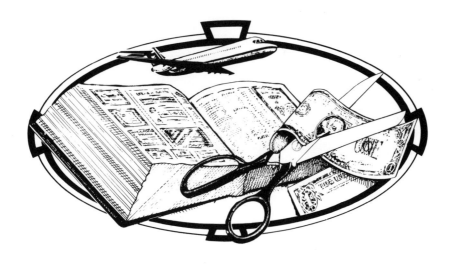

This book is for people who love to do interesting things and go to new places—and don't mind saving money while they're doing it. It is a guide to the perks, privileges, discounts, and special adventures to which you have become entitled simply because you've been around for 50 years or more.

On your 50th birthday (or on your 60th, 62nd, or 65th), you qualify for hundreds of special opportunities and money-saving offers that will have lots of people wishing they were older. All for a couple of good reasons. First, you deserve them, having successfully negotiated your way through life's white waters. And second, as the fastest-growing segment of the American population, you represent an enormous market of potential consumers, a fact that has become quite apparent to the business community. More than a quarter of the U.S. population today is over 50, and that figure is expected to grow by 50 percent in the next 30 years. Almost 13 out of every 100 Americans are now over 65, outnumbering teenagers for the first time in history. Besides, life expectancy is higher today than ever before, and most of us can expect to live a long, healthy, and active life.

Those of us over 50 control most of the nation's wealth, including half of the discretionary income, the money that's left over after essentials have been taken care of, and 80 percent of the savings. Very often, the children have gone, the mortgage has been paid off, the house is fully furnished, the goal of leaving a large inheritance is not a major concern, and the freedom years have arrived at last.

As a group, we're markedly different from previous older generations who pinched pennies and saved them all. We, too, know the value of a dollar, but we feel freer to spend our money because we're better off than our predecessors, a significant number of us having accumulated enough resources to be reasonably secure. We also are far better educated than those before us, and we have developed many more interests and activities.

And, most important, we as a group are remarkably fit, healthy, and energetic. We are in *very* good shape—and feel that way. In fact, a survey has shown that most of us feel at least 15 years younger than our chronological age.

The business community is actively courting the mature market, as we are known, because now we have the time and the money to do all the things we've always put off. Because of the recognition of our numbers, our flexible schedules, and our vast buying power, we are finally being taken very seriously. To get our attention, we are increasingly presented with some real breaks and good deals, all of which are detailed on these pages. We are also invited on trips and adventures specifically oriented toward our interests, needs, and abilities. You will find them here too.

In this book, you will learn how to get what's coming to you—the discounts and privileges you absolutely couldn't get if you were younger:

▶ Discounts at hotels and motels, at car-rental agencies, on buses, trains, and boats

▶ Price breaks on airfares from almost every airline

▶ Colleges and universities that offer you an education for free—or nearly

▶ Insurance companies with discounts for people at 50 or thereabouts

▶ Travel adventures all over the world designed specifically for older travelers

▶ Clubs, trips, and services for mature singles

▶ Ski resorts where you can ski for half price—or for nothing

▶ Tennis tournaments, golf vacations, bike tours, and senior softball leagues designed for you

▶ And much more!

Because every community has its own special perks to offer you, make a practice of *asking* if there are breaks to which you are entitled wherever you go, from movies to museums, concerts to historic sites, hotels to ski resorts, restaurants to riverboats, in this country and abroad. Don't expect clerks or ticket agents, tour operators, restaurant hosts, even travel agents to volunteer them to you. First of all, they may not think of it. Second, they may not realize you have reached the appropriate birthday. And third, they may not want to call attention to your age, just in case that's not something you would appreciate!

Remember to request your privileges *before* you pay or when you order or make reservations, and always carry proof of age or an over-50-club membership card, or, better yet, both. Sometimes the advantages come with membership, but usually they are available to anyone over a specified age.

To make sure you're getting a legitimate discount when you want to take advantage of your over-50 privileges, call the hotel, airline, car-rental company, or tour operator and ask what the regular or normal prices are. Then decide whether you are getting a good deal. And, most important, always ask for *the lowest available rate* and compare that to your discounted rate. Sometimes you'll find that even better specials are available to you.

With the help of this guidebook, you will have a wonderful time and save money too.

Chapter Two
Travel: Making Your Age Pay Off

People over 50 are the most ardent travelers of all. They travel more often, farther, more extravagantly, and for longer periods of time than anybody else. Ever since the travel industry discovered these facts, it's been after our business.

It's fallen in love with our age group because we have more discretionary income than people of other ages. And because we are wonderfully flexible. Many of us no longer have children in school, so we're free to travel at off-peak times or whenever we feel the need for a change of scenery. In fact, we much prefer spring and fall to summer. Some of us have retired, and others have such good jobs that we can make our own schedules. We can even take advantage of midweek slack times when the industry is eager to fill space.

But, best of all, we are energetic, and we're not about to stay home too much. People over 50 account for about one-third of all domestic travel, air trips, hotel/motel nights, and trips to Europe and Africa. Nine out of ten of us are experienced travelers and savvy consumers.

Contrary to what a younger person might think, people in the mature generation aren't content with watching the action. Instead, we like to get right into the middle of it. There's not a place we won't go or an activity we won't try. Though many of us prefer escorted tours, almost half of us choose to travel independently.

Not only that, but we're shrewd—we look for the best deals to the best places. We are experienced comparison shoppers and seek the most for our money.

For all these reasons, we are now offered astonishing numbers of travel-related discounts and reduced rates as well as special tour packages and other perks. Many agencies and tour operators have designed all or at least part of their trips for a mature clientele. Others include older travelers with everyone else but offer us special privileges.

Most airlines sell senior coupon books, good for a year, that let us travel much more cheaply than other people and, in addition, give those of us over 62 a 10 percent reduction on regular fares. And almost all of the hotel and motel chains—as well as individual inns and hotels—now offer similar inducements, such as discounts on rooms and restaurants.

There are so many good deals and great adventures available to you when you are on the move that we'll start right off with travel.

But, first, keep in mind:

▶ Rates, trips, and privileges tend to change at a moment's notice, so check out each of them before you make your plans. Airlines and car-rental agencies are particularly capricious, and it's hard to tell what they offer from one week to the next. The good deals in this guidebook are those that are available as we go to press.

▶ Always ask for your discount when you make your reservations or at the time of purchase, order, or check-in. If you wait until you're checking out or set-tling your bill, it may be too late.

▶ Also remember that discounts may apply only between certain hours, on certain days of the week, or during specific seasons of the year. Research this before mak-ing reservations and always remind the clerk of the discount when you check in or pay your fare. Be flexi-ble when you can and travel during the hours, days, or seasons when you can get the best deals.

▶ It's particularly important when traveling to carry identification with proof of age or membership in a senior club. In most cases, a driver's license or pass-port does the job. So, in some cases, does the organiza-tion's membership card, a birth certificate, a resident alien card, or any other official document showing your date of birth. If you're old enough for a Medicare card or Senior ID card, use that.

▶ Don't always spring for the senior discount without checking out other rates. Sometimes special promo-tional discounts available to anybody any age turn out to be better deals. The car-rental companies and rail-roads, for example, are famous for this. Ask your travel agent or the ticket seller to figure out the *lowest possible available rate* for you at that moment.

▶ If you belong to an organization like AARP, some of these bargains are yours at age 50. Others come along a little later at varying birthdays, so watch for the cutoff points. Also, in many cases, if the person pur-chasing the ticket or trip is the right age, the rest of the party, a traveling companion, or the people sharing the room are entitled to the same reduced rates.

Chapter Three
Out-of-the-Ordinary Escapades

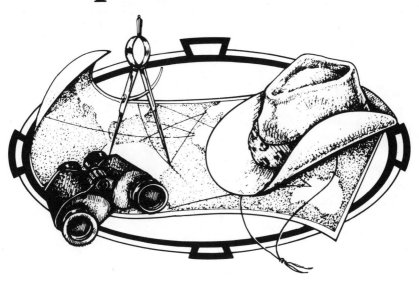

I f you are an intrepid, energetic, perhaps even coura-
geous sort of person who's intrigued by adventures
that don't tempt the usual mature traveler, take a
look at these great possibilities. They are all designed to
give you tales with which to regale your friends, rela-
tives, and acquaintances—at least until you embark on
the next one.

ALASKA WILDLAND ADVENTURES

For close encounters with wildlife and scenery, check out
AWA's Senior Safaris, which take you on tours of Alaska's backcountry escorted by naturalist guides. The
eight-day trips, scheduled weekly during the summer
months, include a salmon bake, a whale-watching cruise,
van tours through national parks and refuges, visits to
historic bush towns, a float trip, and a ride on the Alaska
Railroad. The trips, limited to 18 people, start and end
in Anchorage. If you belong to a recognized senior organization, you will get a $50 discount. Other discounts are
available too, depending on when you travel and how
early you book your trip.

For information: Alaska Wildland Adventures, PO Box
389, Girdwood, AK 99587; 800-334-8730.

ALL ADVENTURE TRAVEL

All Adventure Travel specializes in active vacations: biking, hiking, paddling, snorkeling, diving, kayaking, small-ship cruises, and cultural tours. It represents over 100 tour operators (some of which are listed separately in this book) and offers hundreds of adventurous and off-the-beaten-path trips everywhere in the world, including this continent. The agency will tell you about trips designed specifically for over-50s as well as those eminently suitable for older travelers although not necessarily limited to them.

For information: All Adventure Travel, 5589 Arapahoe, Ste. 208, Boulder, CO 80303; 800-537-4025.

AMERICAN WILDERNESS EXPERIENCE

If you love adventure travel and enjoy roughing it in style, consider the many trips from AWE, one of the country's oldest brokers of adventure travel and dude ranch vacations. Although its offerings are open to all ages, people over 54 get a 5 to 10 percent discount on some trips. For example, several of the horseback pack trips through wilderness areas are offered at slightly reduced senior rates, as are other adventures such as llama trekking and combination trips that may mix riding, rock climbing, biking, and rafting all in one week. Other trips feature special departures and soft adventure itineraries that are specially designed for "prime timers."

For information: American Wilderness Experience, Inc., PO Box 1486, Boulder, CO 80306; 800-444-0099 or 303-444-2622.

CREATIVE ADVENTURE CLUB

This agency offers 15-day soft adventures to South America and the Asia/Pacific area, including Thailand, Borneo, Malaysia, Nepal, Australia, and New Guinea. The exotic trips are designed to go at a pace that's relaxed enough to suit most mature travelers and often include activities such as snorkeling, hiking, mountain trekking, caving, and train tours as well as basic sightseeing. Some of the tours are specifically for seniors, while others include all ages.

For information: Creative Adventure Club, 3007 Royce Lane, Costa Mesa, CA 92626; 800-544-5088.

HOSTELLING INTERNATIONAL/AMERICAN YOUTH HOSTELS

The organization that sends teenagers on low-cost biking and hiking trips all over the world is not for youth alone. In fact, it offers an array of inexpensive adventures called Discovery Tours, some specifically for people over 50. And, of course, older people are invited to go along on any trips labeled "open" or "adult."

If you want to go on a Discovery Tour, you must become a member of HI/AYH. Membership for adults is $25 a year, unless you've reached 55, in which case you pay only $15. Members get a card, a guidebook that lists hostels in the United States and Canada, and access to any Hostelling International facility worldwide. You may purchase handbooks for Europe and other parts of the world.

The United States affiliate of the International Youth Hostel Federation that coordinates more than 5,000 hostels in 70 countries, HI/AYH has been operating for over half a century. Each of its trips is limited to 10 participants, including the trip leader. You'll sleep at base camps that are usually hostels—inexpensive dormitory-style accommodations, no two of them alike. You might stay in a castle in Germany or a lighthouse in California or a former dude ranch in Colorado. Most hostels have kitchens where your group prepares its own meals, although a few have cafeterias.

Each year, HI/AYH plans several itineraries for the over-50 crowd, usually van-supported hiking tours with day hikes from base camps. Recent rosters have offered hiking trips in New Mexico; Alaska's national parks; Rocky Mountain, Grand Teton, and Yellowstone National Parks; the Northwest coast; and Canada's Banff, Jasper, and Yoho National Parks.

In addition to all that, members are entitled to lodge at any hostel in the world, including the new network of urban hostels now in Washington, D.C., New York, Boston, San Francisco, Miami Beach, New Orleans, Los Angeles, and Honolulu. One night's stay costs $5 to $22. There is no maximum age limitation for booking a bed in these wonderfully cheap lodgings and hobnobbing with other hostelers who prefer not to pay exorbitant hotel prices. Be ready, however, to sleep in a double-decker cot in a sex-segregated dormitory for six or eight people supervised by "hostel parents." Many hostels have family or couple rooms that can be reserved in advance.

For information: HI/AYH, Dept. 855, 733 15th St. NW, Ste. 840, Washington, DC 20005; 202-783-6161.

HOSTELLING INTERNATIONAL—CANADA

A network of about 80 hostels throughout the Canadian provinces, HI-Canada offers members of all ages an inexpensive night's sleep in a wide variety of places ranging from historic homes and refurbished jails and courthouses to log cabins in the mountains. Located in all major gateway cities and also in remote locations, your accommodations—shared, simple, and quite basic—cost an average of $15 (Canadian) a night. Membership costs $26.75 (Canadian) per year and allows you to use any HI facility worldwide.

For information: Hostelling International—Canada, 205 Catherine St., Ste. 400, Ottawa, ON K2P 1C3; 613-237-7884.

MT. ROBSON ADVENTURE HOLIDAYS

For people over 50 who crave action and the wilderness, this agency plans a couple of "gentle adventures" every summer in British Columbia's Mt. Robson Provincial Park, just west of Jasper. Mt. Robson is the highest mountain in the Canadian Rockies, and the park offers spectacular scenery. The Fifty Plus Adventure is a four-night package trip for up to 10 participants that includes a guided trek, a nature tour, a marshlands canoe trip, and a gentle rafting float trip. You sleep in heated log cabins at the base camp and eat three hardy meals a day. The five-night Helicamping Adventure flies you to a remote mountain lake where you spend three nights tenting and, led by an experienced guide, take day hikes into the surrounding alpine areas.

For information: Mt. Robson Adventure Holidays, PO Box 687, Valemount, BC V0E 2Z0; 604-566-4386.

OUTWARD BOUND

Famous for its wilderness trips for youngsters, with a goal of building self-confidence, self-esteem, and the ability to work as a team, Outward Bound also offers short and popular courses specifically for people who are at least 40 years old and often many years beyond that. The physical activities are less strenuous than they are for the 16-year-olds, but participants are expected to push themselves beyond their self-imposed physical and mental limits. Some of the courses focus on helping people effect a smooth transition from career to retirement.

The six- to eight-day courses designed especially for older participants include backpacking in the southern Appalachians and canoeing or sailing along the Maine coast. You'll sleep in a sleeping bag in a tent or under a tarp and cook your own food. You must be in good health, but you needn't be an experienced camper.

For information: Outward Bound USA, Route 9D, R2 Box 280, Garrison, NY 10524-9757; 800-243-8520 or in New York, 914-424-4000.

THE OVER THE HILL GANG

The Gang is a club that welcomes fun-loving, adventurous, peppy people over 50 who are looking for action and contemporaries to pursue it with. No naps, no rockers, no sitting by the pool sipping planter's punch. The Over the Hill Gang started as a ski club many years ago but now is into lots of different activities, including travel (see Chapters 13 and 14 for more about the club). All sports-oriented, recent trips have included skiing at

Keystone, Taos, Steamboat, Aspen, Vail, and other ski areas in the West, New Zealand, Austria's Alps, and the Canadian Rockies; whitewater rafting on Idaho's Salmon River; and biking on Cape Cod.

Join the national organization for $37 ($60 per couple) and, if there is a chapter in your area, you may join it too for small additional yearly dues. You'll never lack for company and interesting places to go.

For information: Over the Hill Gang International, 3310 Cedar Heights Dr., Colorado Springs, CO 80904; 719-685-4656.

RIVER ODYSSEYS WEST

Scheduling many "magical adventures on rivers, trails, and seas," ROW reserves two whitewater river trips a year exclusively for over-50s. For three or five days in the summer, the Prime Time trip takes you down the last 53 miles of the Salmon River in Idaho plus another 21 miles on the Snake River, floating through four different volcanic canyons and stopping at historic sites. Traveling in rubber rafts powered by an oarsperson, you sleep in tents on sandy beaches.

Also for mature travelers only is a 12-day sailing trip along Turkey's southern coast on a traditional Turkish *gulet*, a 72-foot wooden motor/sail yacht. The leisurely voyage leaves time for visiting fishing villages, beaches, and Greek, Roman, and Byzantine ruins ashore.

For information: River Odysseys West, PO Box 579-UD, Coeur d'Alene, ID 83816-0579; 800-451-6034 or 208-765-0841.

SENIOR WORLD TOURS

Planning its trips expressly for mature travelers, Senior World Tours offers not only a winter snowmobiling holiday but also several other adventurous and athletic excursions. It plans, for example, walking trips in Jackson Hole, Wyoming; England's famous Cotswolds; Vermont; and the Olympic Peninsula of Washington State; plus a biking and heli-hiking trip in the Canadian Rockies.

For information: Senior World Tours, 3701 Buttrick Rd. SE, Ada, MI 49301-9221; 800-676-5801 or 616-676-5885.

WARREN RIVER EXPEDITIONS

Warren River Expeditions offers seniors-only whitewater raft trips down Idaho's Salmon River, the longest undammed river in the country—fast and wild in the spring, tame and gentle in late summer. You'll float through unique ecosystems, down the deep Salmon River Canyon, and through the Frank Church Wilderness Area, where you'll view the lush scenery and the abundant wildlife. Planned as soft adventure trips for people who are not enthusiastic about sleeping on the ground, the six-day senior trips put you up each night in comfortable backcountry lodges. Want to take the trip with your grandchildren? There is a grandparents expedition once every summer. Over-50 readers of this book get a 10 percent discount on the cost of any of this agency's adventures, so mention it.

For information: Warren River Expeditions, PO Box 1375, Salmon, ID 83467-1375; 800-765-0421 or 208-756-6387.

INTERGENERATIONAL ADVENTURES

AMERICAN MUSEUM OF NATURAL HISTORY FAMILY TOURS

This famous museum now runs educational trips for children (12 and up) accompanied by parents or grandparents. Currently listed among its family tours are a cruise on the waterways of Russia, a trip to the Galapagos Islands, a winter holidays safari in Kenya, and a Mediterranean cruise from Italy to Turkey and Greece. Groups are led by lecturers from the museum.

For information: Discovery Tours, American Museum of Natural History, Central Park West at 79th St., New York, NY 10024; 800-462-8687 or 212-769-5700.

DELTA QUEEN GRANDPARENTS PROGRAM

On two cruises aboard the *Mississippi Queen* in November and December, the Delta Queen Steamboat Company provides a free cabin for two children under 18 when they travel with grandparents who purchase their stateroom at full fare. Many of the activities and tours are designed by the Grandparent Connection to be shared by both generations. In addition, an onboard seminar series for grandparents covers such topics as keeping connected with grandchildren who live far away and investing safely for children's future. Daily classes for all are also offered on the history of the region, the steamboats, the river, and the interesting ports of call such as Natchez and Vicksburg. The cruises—one for five nights, the other for seven—are roundtrip out of New Orleans.

For information: The Delta Queen Steamboat Co., 30 Robin Street Wharf, New Orleans, LA 70130-1890; 800-458-6789.

ELDERHOSTEL

Elderhostel, the well-known educational travel organization for people over 60 and mates over 50, now offers a number of intergenerational programs—some for Elderhostelers and their adult children, some for members and their grandchildren or other young friends. All of them are designed to give you a good time while you enjoy one another's company unhassled by everyday pressures. The offerings vary from season to season, but some of the recent programs were held at Yosemite Institute in Yosemite National Park; Western Montana College in Dillon, in the shadow of the Rocky Mountains; Wolf Ridge Environmental Learning Center, overlooking Lake Superior in Minnesota; and Strathcona Park Lodge, on Vancouver Island in British Columbia.

For information: Elderhostel, 75 Federal St., Boston, MA 02110; 617-426-7788. In Canada: Elderhostel Canada, 308 Wellington St., Kingston ON K7K 7A7; 613-530-2222.

FAMILYHOSTEL

FamilyHostel is an international travel and learning program for families—parents, grandparents, and children (8 to 15)—sponsored by University of New Hampshire Continuing Education, which also runs the Interhostel program for adults over 50 (see Chapter 16). It takes families to foreign countries where, separately and together, they attend presentations and classes led by faculty from local educational institutions, go on field trips to contemporary and historic sites, attend social/ cultural events, and enjoy recreational activities for all generations. Family-style accommodations are in residence halls, university apartments, or hotels. Offered in the summer months in Europe, Australia, and Mexico, programs vary in length from 10 days to three weeks. The moderate cost includes airfare, meals, accommodations, and activities.

For information: FamilyHostel, University of New Hampshire, 6 Garrison Ave., Durham, NH 03824; 800-733-9753.

GOOD LIFE GRANDTOURS

If you live anywhere near Lincoln, Nebraska, you may want to sign yourself and your grandchildren (9 to 14) up for one of this agency's two- and three-day tours for grandparents and kids. The itineraries vary from season to season, but current trips take you to Kansas, Omaha, Minneapolis, and other interesting places.

For information: Good Life Tours, 8200 Fletcher Ave., Lincoln, NE 68507; 800-233-0404 or 402-467-2900.

GRANDEXPLORERS

GrandExplorers, recently created by the B'nai B'rith Center for Jewish Family Life, is designed to help grandparents pass on family traditions and heritage to their grandchildren, instilling Jewish values and identity in an age when family members tend to live far apart. Its major program is a 10-day vacation in Israel that includes stays in Jerusalem and Tel Aviv, a jeep tour of the Golan Heights, an archaeological dig, visits to historic sites throughout Israel, and two nights on a kibbutz.

For information: GrandExplorers, B'nai B'rith Israel Commission, 1640 Rhode Island Ave. NW, Washington, DC 20036; 800-500-6533 or 202-857-6577.

GRANDPARENT/GRANDCHILD SUMMER CAMP

Take your grandchild to camp with you for a week this summer. The mission of this camp, led by the Foundation for Grandparenting and planned especially for families whose members don't live next door, is to bring the two generations together by giving them the time and space to be alone together, escape from the demands of the everyday world, experience the power and joy of their bond, and have fun. The site is the Sagamore Institute, a former Vanderbilt "great camp" in the Adirondack region of New York.

In the mornings, campers engage in joint activities such as walks, berrypicking, group games, and nature art. In the afternoons, the age groups are on their own, free to choose from many recreational activities. Before dinner, grandparents meet for discussions of their own issues, and in the evenings everyone gets together for stories, campfires, singalongs, square dancing, or other activities.

For information: Sagamore Institute, Sagamore Rd., Raquette Lake, NY 13436; 315-354-5311.

GRANDPARENTS/GRANDKIDS WESTERN CAMP

The College of the Tehachapis, a unique continuing education institution in California, presents three six-day sleepaway camp sessions for grandparents and their grandchildren (aged 6 to 12) in the summer months. Both generations of campers lodge in cottage units at Sky Mountain Resort in nearby Stallion Springs and enjoy educational/recreational programs in science, nature, arts and crafts, and sports. The modest cost covers all lodging, meals, and programs. Here's another good opportunity to enjoy your grandchildren in a relaxed way.

For information: COTT, PO Box 1911-61, Tehachapi, CA 93581; 800-224-8115 or 805-823-8115.

GRANDTRAVEL

Grandtravel was the first agency to offer special trips for grandparents and their grandchildren so they can share the pleasures of traveling together. Grandtravel's series of itineraries, scheduled for normal school breaks, aims to appeal to both generations. It includes trips to Washington, D.C., or Alaska; tours through the American Southwest, northern California, or New England; a Hawaiian tour; African safaris; visits to Israel, Australia, Ireland, England, Scotland, Switzerland, and France; a tour of national parks; and barge trips in Holland. Grandtravel will also arrange for independent grandparent/grandchild travel, family groups, or school-sponsored groups.

Actually, you don't have to be a grandparent to take the trips—aunts, uncles, cousins, godparents, and other surrogate grannies are welcome. Ranging from 7 to 18 days, the tours, led by teacher-escorts, include good hotels with recreation facilities, transportation by motorcoach with rest stops every two hours, games, talks, music on the buses, and a travel manual for every tour. Each trip provides time for the older folks and the children to be alone with their own age group. The kids may go roller skating and dine on fried chicken—supervised, of course—while the grandparents do something grown up, such as going to a gourmet restaurant for dinner.
For information: Grandtravel, The Ticket Counter, 6900 Wisconsin Ave., Chevy Chase, MD 20815; 800-247-7651 or 301-986-0790.

OUTDOOR VACATIONS FOR WOMEN OVER 40
For a multigenerational adventure trip, check out the offerings of this unusual agency that specializes in vacations for groups of women who love the outdoors. Several of its weekend trips out of Boston are designed specifically for mothers, daughters, grandmothers, granddaughters, aunts, and nieces who want to spend time together. At least two generations must be represented, with one participant over 40 and the other over 21. Among the current multigenerational opportunities are three-day windjammer cruises off the coast of Maine and hiking trips in New Hampshire.

For information: Outdoor Vacations for Women Over 40, PO Box 200, Groton, MA 01450; 508-448-3331.

RASCALS IN PARADISE

Specializing in family vacations for parents and children, Rascals in Paradise also invites grandparents and grandchildren to go along on its adventure trips to such places as Mexico and the Caribbean, the Bahamas, Europe, New Zealand, the South Pacific, Africa, the Galapagos Islands, Hawaii, and ranches in the West. All group trips, three to six families per group, include an escort who plans activities for the older children and a baby-sitter for the little ones. This agency will plan independent vacations, too, as well as family reunions and multigenerational celebrations.

For information: Rascals in Paradise, 650 Fifth St., Ste. 505, San Francisco, CA 94107; 800-872-7225 or 415-978-9800.

R.F.D. TRAVEL

If you're looking for new traveling companions, consider your grandchildren. This agency schedules a few trips for the two generations every summer, always featuring special attractions for the kids. Right now the itineraries include an American Heritage Tour that takes the travelers from Philadelphia to Washington, D.C., stopping all along the way; a three-day Oregon Trail Wagon Trek

in Nebraska; and six days exploring New York City.
For information: R.F.D. Travel, 5201 Johnson Dr., Mission, KS 66205; 800-365-5359.

VISTA TOURS

The GrandVista tours from Vista Tours have two grandparent/grandchildren itineraries every summer. A seven-day South Dakota bus tour includes visits to Rapid City, Mount Rushmore, the Badlands, and Custer State Park; and a five-day bus trip to Reno and Lake Tahoe includes the Ponderosa Ranch, Virginia City, and Donner Summit. Activities are planned for the two generations separately and together, with a goal of bringing everyone closer through shared experiences.
For information: Vista Tours, 1923 N. Carson St., Ste. 105, Carson City, NV 89701; 800-248-4782.

WARREN RIVER EXPEDITIONS

Every summer, this tour operator offers a Grandparents/Grandkids raft trip down Idaho's Salmon River, a great way for the two generations to spend time together. You stay in rustic lodges along the way. See the Warren River Expeditions entry earlier in this chapter for more about this adventure.
For information: Warren River Expeditions, PO Box 1375, Salmon, ID 83467-1375; 800-765-0421 or 208-756-6387.

Chapter Four
Cutting Your Costs Abroad

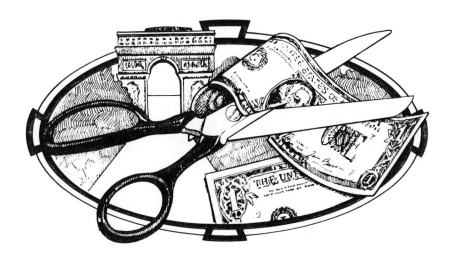

The most enthusiastic voyagers of all age groups, Americans over 50—one out of three adults and a quarter of the total population—spend more time and money on travel than anybody else, especially when it comes to going abroad. It's been estimated that more than 4 out of every 10 passport holders are at least 55 years old. And there's hardly a country in the world today that doesn't actively encourage mature travelers to come for a visit, because everybody has discovered that they are travel's biggest potential market.

Because you are currently being hotly pursued, you as well as local residents can take advantage of many good deals in other lands. Railroad systems in most European countries, for example, offer deep discounts to seniors that are especially valuable if you plan an extended stay in one place. This chapter gives you a rundown on these and other ways to cut your European holiday costs, especially if you are planning your trip on your own. For the U.S. and Canada, see Chapter 9.

But, first, keep in mind:

▶ Always ask about senior savings when you travel on trains, buses, or boats anywhere in the world. Do the same when you buy tickets for movies, theater, museums, tours, sightseeing sites, historic buildings, and attractions. Don't assume, simply because you haven't heard about them or the ticket agent hasn't mentioned them, that they don't exist. They are becoming more and more common everywhere.

▶ Some countries require that you purchase a senior card to take advantage of senior discounts, but most simply require proof of age, usually in the form of a passport.

▶ Always have your necessary identification with you and be ready to show it. Occasionally you may need an extra passport photograph.

▶ For specifics on a country's senior discounts, call its national tourist office. Or call Rail Europe (800-438-7245), which represents most European railways, for information about train passes.

▶ Your passport may be required along with your rail pass while you are in transit, so keep it with you.

FINDING A DOCTOR OVERSEAS

Before you leave on a trip to foreign lands, it would be wise to send for a list of physicians all over the world who speak English or French, have had medical training in Great Britain, the U.S., or Canada, and have agreed to reasonable preset fees. When you join the free nonprofit International Association for Medical Assistance to Travellers (IAMAT), you will get a membership card entitling you to services and its prearranged rates, a directory of physicians in 125 countries and territories, a clinical record to take along with you, advice on immunizations and preventive measures, and information on sanitary conditions in 450 cities.
For information: IAMAT, 417 Center St., Lewiston, NY 14092; 716-754-4883.

EUROPE BY RAIL

EURAILPASS, EUROPASS, SCANRAIL

The **Eurailpass** is good for free unlimited first-class train travel in 17 European countries (including Ireland but not Great Britain). There is no senior discount on the pass but it is certainly worth considering if you plan to cover many miles in several countries. (On the other hand, if you are visiting just one country, you'd be better off taking advantage of that nation's senior discounts.) Available for various numbers of days up to three months, the Eurailpass gets you free or reduced rates on many buses, ferries, and steamers. Traveling with a group of three or more people (or two or more in the off-season) and thereby qualifying for a **Eurail Saverpass** is an even better deal. Remember that you must buy your passes before leaving home—they are not available overseas.

The brand-new **Europass** is another option. It's good for unlimited first-class train travel for 5 to 15 days (which need not be consecutive) in three to five western European countries. Again there's no senior discount on this pass but it is a good value for people who plan to travel in France, Germany, Italy, Spain, and Switzerland within a two-month period.

Scanrail 55+ Pass, also available only on this side of the Atlantic, gives you unlimited travel in four Scandinavian countries: Denmark, Finland, Norway, and Sweden. This pass, unlike Eurail and Europass, costs you less than younger travelers if you are 55 or more. For details, see Scandinavian Countries in this chapter. **For information:** Rail Europe, 2100 Central Ave., Boulder, CO 80301; 800-4-EURAIL (800-438-7245).

COUNTRY-BY-COUNTRY TRAVEL DEALS

AUSTRIA

You may buy tickets at half price for travel on Austrian Federal Railways and the bus system of the Federal Railways and the Postal Service (except on municipal transit lines) once you have a Railway Senior Citizens ID Card. You must be 60 if you are a woman, or 65 if you are a man, to purchase the card at any railroad station, including those in gateway cities in Germany and at some post offices in Austria. Take proof of your age (your passport) and an extra passport-size photo. The card is good for the calendar year and currently costs approximately $27. It is not available in the U.S., but you may send for it by mail.

If you are going to be in Austria for only a short time, however, pick up a Vienna Card when you arrive in that fabulous city. It is available in hotels and tourist information offices and costs ATS 180, or about $18. With the card, you may use all forms of public transportation within the city limits for three days from its first use and get reduced admission to museums, concerts, and sightseeing attractions and tours as well as some shopping discounts. An informative booklet comes with the card.

For information: Austrian National Tourist Office, PO Box 1142, New York, NY 10108-1142; 212-944-6880.

BELGIUM

Travelers over the age of 60 may buy a Golden Rail Pass, available only in Belgium, that gives you seven free train trips within the country for 1,990 Belgian francs (about $62 at this writing), first class, or 1,290 francs (about $40), second class. If you plan only a short trip, however, a better choice may be the Belgian Half-Fare Card (550 francs), available to anyone any age and valid for a month. It allows you to travel on all trains for half price.

For information: Belgian National Tourist Office, 780 Third Ave., New York, NY 10017; 212-758-8130.

BERMUDA

February is Golden Rendezvous Month in Bermuda, a time when special activities, entertainment, and discounts are reserved for visitors over 50. Hotels offer special packages, golf courses sponsor tournaments, and the Bermuda Bridge Club invites you to play. There are lectures on such topics as Bermudian traditions, flora and fauna, and architecture and tours to interesting sites on the island. Pick up two free ferry/bus tokens and a coupon book of discounts at a Visitors Services Bureau. And consider buying Bermuda's $20 transportation pass that provides unlimited use of ferries and buses for three days, available at the Hamilton Bus Terminal and at Visitors Services Bureaus. By the way, 29 major hotels guarantee a 10 percent discount on the room rates for the days in January, February, and March when the temperature does not reach a minimum of 68 degrees.

For information: Bermuda Department of Tourism, 310 Madison Ave., New York, NY 10017; 800-223-6106.

FRANCE

The two varieties of Carte Vermeil, issued specifically for travelers over 60 regardless of nationality, entitle you to purchase rail tickets on the French National Railroad (SNCF) for half price in either first or second class. The Carte Vermeil Quatre Temps, which costs 135 francs at this writing, allows for four reduced-fare rail trips within one year. The Carte Vermeil Plein Temps, at 255 francs, gives you unlimited rail travel at half price for a year. Not sold in the U.S., both cards may be purchased at major railroad stations throughout France. Be sure to have proof of your age (passport or driver's license) with you. The half fare applies only during the "période bleue": from noon on Saturday until 3 P.M. on Sunday and from Monday noon until Friday noon. At other times, you'll get only a 20 percent discount. It is not valid on certain blackout days during major holiday periods. There is no Carte Vermeil discount on the Paris suburban train network.

What's more, with the Plein Temps card you will get 30 percent off on train tickets from France to most other European countries.

Not only are train fares cut in half but if you are 60-plus you can also get greatly reduced fares (usually 40 to 60 percent off the full fares) on most flights on the domestic airline Air Inter, which serves 31 cities in

France. And don't forget your 10 percent senior discount on Air France (see Chapter 7).

And, of course, always check out the senior rates at museums, movies, and other cultural activities, where anyone over 60, French or foreign, gets half price.

For information: French Government Tourist Office, 610 Fifth Ave., New York, NY 10020; 212-757-1125.

GERMANY

Travelers over 60 who plan long stays in Germany may profit by buying a BahnCard, valid for one year, for half the regular price. With it in hand, they may then purchase half-price tickets for long-distance rail travel within the republic. The BahnCard currently costs 220 DM for senior travelers. Not sold in the U.S. or Canada, the card may be purchased at any major railroad station in Germany. For short trips and shorter stays, however, the German RailPass, not discounted for older travelers, is probably a better bet. Buy it here before you go.

For information: Call your travel agent or DER Tours at 800-782-2424.

GREAT BRITAIN

Here's where you're going to get some of the best bargains in Europe, because the British are really into "the very good years," by which they usually mean over 60. There are discounts and special rates on just about everything—railroads, airlines, hotels, museums, day cruises, theaters, and historical and tourist sites.

The BritRail Senior Pass and the Senior Flexipass (for travelers 60 and over) give you reduced rates for consecutive days on 8-day, 15-day, 22-day, or 1-month passes, first class or standard, for unlimited travel in England, Scotland, and Wales. The rates are even better than with the regular BritRail Pass, which is a bargain for everyone else. The Senior Flexipass is the same idea but allows unlimited rail travel on 4, 8, or 15 days out of one month. The pass must be purchased through your travel agent *before* you leave this continent—it is not sold in Britain. By the way, the Eurailpass is not accepted in Great Britain.

In Northern Ireland, you may wish to avail yourself of a Rail Runabout ticket that gives you seven days of unlimited travel on all scheduled rail services at half price. You must be 65 for this privilege. The Freedom of Northern Ireland tickets do the same on all scheduled bus services except coach tours. Choose a one-day or a seven-day ticket.

People of other ages need the Britexpress Card for one-third off the fare throughout England, Scotland, and Wales on express buses operated by the National Express Bus Company and Scottish Citylink Coaches—but you don't. That's because you automatically get a one-third reduction on any bus fare simply by showing proof of your age.

Be sure to buy a Great British Heritage Pass, again before you leave home. It gets you free admission to more than 600 castles, palaces, and manor homes and gardens in England, Scotland, and Wales.

If you're going to spend much time in London, buy the London Visitor Travelcard through your travel agent here in the U.S. With it, you will get unlimited rides on the city's bus and underground systems as well as tube travel to and from Heathrow Airport for three, four, or seven consecutive days.

Most theaters offer senior discounts, although sometimes only for matinees. Check at the box office or ask the hotel concierge.

Hotels may also give senior discounts in the off-season (November through March), so always inquire when you make your reservations.

For information: British Tourist Authority, 551 5th Ave., Ste. 701, New York, NY 10176; 800-462-2748 or 212-986-2200.

For rail passes: BritRail, 1500 Broadway, New York, NY 10036; 800-677-8585 or 212-575-2667. In Canada: 800-387-7245 or 416-482-9196.

MAKING FRIENDS BY MAIL

International Pen Friends is a pen-pal organization with members all over the world. Anybody any age is eligible to join (the membership fee is slightly less if you're over 60) and be matched up with pen friends in other countries—an excellent way to make interesting contacts or practice a foreign language and to have friends to visit when you travel. You receive a list of 14 names of people who are in your age group and share your interests, in a choice of countries and/or languages. There are currently about 300,000 IPF members in 188 countries.

For information: Send a self-addressed, stamped envelope to International Pen Friends, PO Box 290065, Homecrest Station, Brooklyn, NY 11229.

GREECE

Here, if you are 60, male or female, you may buy a Hellenic Railways pass that's good for five single train trips within Greece. When you've used up your five trips, you may travel on trains and buses at half price. Valid for one year, the pass may be purchased at any major railroad station in Greece. The only hitch: there are some blackout periods when the card doesn't do the trick—from July 1 to the end of September, plus the 10 days before and after Easter and Christmas.

For information: Greek National Tourist Organization, 645 Fifth Ave., New York, NY 10022; 212-421-5777.

HONG KONG

Stop at a Hong Kong Tourist Association Information Centre in the territory and pick up a copy of *Guide for Travellers Over 60*, a booklet containing information and practical advice for older visitors. It lists the senior discounts (some available at 60, others at 65) offered by hotels, restaurants, shops, museums, and public transport. It also offers organized tours with reduced senior rates. Ask for the "60+ Privilege Card" at the same time.

For information: Hong Kong Tourist Association, 590 Fifth Ave., New York, NY 10036-4706; 212-869-5008.

IRELAND

Many hotels in the Republic of Ireland offer senior discounts, especially off-peak, so make it a policy to inquire about them when you make your reservations. In most cases, you must be 65 to qualify. Theaters (midweek), national monuments, and historic sites give you price reductions too. Always ask.

If you take a CIE motorcoach tour in Ireland, you can take $55 per person off the cost if you are 55, choose certain tours on certain departure dates (those in the "55 'n' Smiling" program), and are among the first 15 passengers to book the trip.

For information: CIE Tours International, 108 Ridgedale Ave., PO Box 2355, Morristown, NJ 07962-2355; 800-CIE-TOUR.

ITALY

The Carta d'Argenta (Silver Card), which currently costs about $30 and is valid for a year, entitles everyone who is 60 or over, tourist or resident, to a 30 percent discount on Italian railways most of the year and a 20 percent discount during the "high season." It can be purchased at railroad stations in Italy at the special windows (Biglietti Speciali). When you buy your tickets, flash the card to get the discount. This will obviously save you money if you plan to travel extensively in Italy, but the Flexi-Rail Pass, sold only in the U.S., or the BTLC, available in both the U.S. and Italy, may prove to be a better value for shorter stays with less mileage. Check them out before making a decision.

For information: CIT Tours, 342 Madison Ave., Suite 207, New York, NY 10173; 800-CIT-TOUR or 212-697-2100.

LUXEMBOURG

Anybody over 65 pays half fare on trains and buses. Just show proof of age when you buy your tickets.

For information: Luxembourg National Tourist Office, 17 Beekman Pl., New York, NY 10022; 212-935-8888.

PORTUGAL

You can travel in Portugal for half fare on interregional trains and for 30 percent on trains between Lisbon and Porto if you are 65 and display your passport to prove it. The only times this offer is not in effect are during rush hours Monday to Friday on the Lisbon suburban lines.

For information: Portuguese National Tourist Office, 590 Fifth Ave., New York, NY 10036; 212-354-4403.

SCANDINAVIAN COUNTRIES

If you are a mature traveler, Scandinavia has some good deals for you. First of all, you may travel in four Scandinavian countries—Denmark, Sweden, Norway, and Finland—less expensively than other people.

One way is to take advantage of the new Scanrail 55+ Pass, which must be purchased in the U.S. before you go. This gives you a pass at discounted prices, if you are 55, for unlimited travel by train in all four countries. You may buy the pass for five days (to be used within 15 days), for 10 days (to be used within a month), or for a month of consecutive days, allowing you to travel wherever you like on the national rail networks. Bonuses (some of which may constitute usage of a travel day) include free passage on several water crossings, half price on several cruise lines, 25 percent discount on certain ferries, and discounts from 10 to 30 percent on hotel room rates during the months of June, July, and August.

For information: Call your travel agent or Rail Europe at 800-438-7245.

Now here are the current country-by-country opportunities for mature travelers:

Denmark: Here you may buy "65-Tickets" for reduced train fares in both first and second class every day of the week, with the fare even less on "cheap days" (Monday through Thursday and Saturday).

Sweden: If you buy the Reslust Card in Sweden, you will get a 25 percent discount on all trains on Tuesdays, Wednesdays, Thursdays, and Saturdays. And you may also take advantage of discounts in dining cars, special summer rates, and more. The card, which currently costs everyone else about $18 (U.S.), costs you (at 65 or older) only $6.

Norway: Norway's offer is half price for a train ticket, first or second class, any time, anywhere. For this, however, you or your spouse must be 67. Also at 67, you become eligible for a discount on Norwegian Coastal Voyages (except in June or July) and, at 60, half price on Color Line cruises to England and the Continent (see Chapter 5).

Finland: The Finnish Senior Citizen Card, available for about $9 (U.S.) at railroad or bus stations, entitles you at age 65 to half fare on trains and 30 percent off on bus trips that are at least 80 kilometers one way. The Silja Line, ships that serve North Sea ports, offers junior rates to seniors.

Also look into the Scandinavian BonusPass. It is not age-oriented but gives discounts of up to 50 percent off the rates at more than a hundred first-class hotels during the summer season and on weekends all year.

And consider picking up a city card—Copenhagen Card, Oslo Card, Helsinki Card, Stockholm Card—at tourist offices, airports, or hotels in the capital cities; cards are also available for Tampere, Finland, and for Gothenburg and Malmo, Sweden. The cards, which now cost about $15 a day, simplify your life in these cities by giving you unlimited travel on city transportation, free entry to museums and attractions, and discounts on sight-seeing tours, hotels, car rentals, restaurants, guided walking tours, and events.

For information: Scandinavian National Tourist Offices, 655 Third Ave., New York, NY 10017; 212-949-2333.

SWITZERLAND

The Swiss Hotel Association will provide, for the asking, a list of over 450 hotels that participate in the "Season for Seniors," giving reduced rates to women over 62 and men over 65 (if you are a couple, only one of you must be the required minimum age). The only catch is that in most cases the lower rates do not apply during peak travel periods, including the summer months.

Although the following travel passes are not just for mature travelers but are available to everyone, they are worth noting because they may save you considerable money on fares:

The first is the Swiss Pass, useful if you are planning to do extensive traveling within the country because it allows you unlimited trips on the Swiss Travel System, including most private and mountain railroads, lake steamers, and most postal motorcoaches, public tramways, and buses in 30 cities. It also lets you buy excursion tickets to mountaintops at 25 percent off. Buy it for 8 days, 15 days, or 1 month.

With the Swiss Flexi Pass you may travel three days during a 15-day period.

And then there's the Swiss Card. Valid for one month, it gives you one free trip from any entry point to your destination within Switzerland and return. In addition, with the Card you may purchase an unlimited number of tickets on all scheduled services by train, postal coach, or lake steamer at half price.

The travel passes are available in the U.S. through your travel agent or Rail Europe. In Switzerland, they are sold at many railroad stations and airports upon showing your passport.

For information: Swiss National Tourist Office, 608 Fifth Ave., New York, NY 10020; 212-757-5944. Or Rail Europe, 2100 Central Ave., Boulder, CO 80301; 800-438-7245.

Chapter Five
Trips and Tours for the Mature Traveler

A few clever over-50 organizations and travel
agencies now cater only to the mature traveler.
They choose destinations sure to appeal to those
who have already seen much of the world, arrange trips
that are leisurely and unhassled, give you congenial
contemporaries to travel with and group hosts to smooth
the way, and provide many special services you never got
before. They also give you a choice between strenuous
action-filled tours and those that are more relaxed. In
fact, most of the agencies offer so many choices that the
major problem becomes making a decision about where
to go.

Options range from cruises in the Caribbean or the
Greek Isles to grand tours of the Orient, sight-seeing
excursions in the United States, trips to the Canadian
Rockies, theater tours of London, African safaris and
snorkeling vacations on the Great Barrier Reef off Australia. There's no place in the world over-50s won't go.

Among the newer and most popular trends are apart-
ment/hotel complexes in American and European resort
areas, as well as apartments in major cities. Here you
can stay put for as long as you like, using the apartment
as a home base for short-range roaming and exploring.

To qualify for some of the trips, one member of the

party must meet the minimum age requirement, while the others may be younger.

TRIPS FOR THE MATURE TRAVELER

AJS TRAVEL CONSULTANTS
The AJS 50 Plus Club specializes in discounted trips for the older generation, all leisurely and escorted. Current offerings include a 17-day tour of Israel, a series of 15-day Spa Tours of Italy, and a choice of 15-day unstructured stay-put vacations in a choice of resort towns in Switzerland. The annual membership fee for the club is $25 (and includes your spouse).
For information: AJS Travel Consultants, 177 Beach 116th St., Rockaway Park, NY 11694; 800-221-5002 or 718-945-5900.

GOLDEN AGE TRAVELLERS
This over-50 club, now celebrating its 26th anniversary, specializes in discounted cruises to just about everywhere in the world but offers land trips at group rates as well. When you join the club ($10 a year or $15 per couple), you will receive a quarterly newsletter with listings of upcoming adventures, discounts, and bonuses on major cruise lines. Other inducements are tour escorts on every venture and credits against the transportation costs to the airport on certain trips. Single travelers may choose to be enrolled in the "Roommates Wanted" list to help them find a companion to share the cabin and the costs.

For members in the San Francisco and Sacramento areas, there are one-day excursions and meetings where you may meet fellow travelers. Especially intriguing to mature travelers are this agency's long-stay trips. On these, you stay put—for example, in Spain, Portugal, Guatemala, Australia, Costa Rica, or Argentina—at the same hotel for two or three weeks, and, if you wish, take short side trips. The packages include air, hotel, and sometimes meals.

For information: Golden Age Travellers, Pier 27, the Embarcadero, San Francisco, CA 94111; 800-258-8880 or 415-563-2361.

GRAND CIRCLE TRAVEL

Grand Circle caters to people over 50 and plans all of its trips exclusively for them. The first U.S. company to market senior travel, it has escorted over 600,000 Americans all over the world.

Grand Circle specializes in Live Abroad Extended Vacations, which let you live in an apartment, villa, or house in a foreign country for 2 to 26 weeks. You have your choice of staying in the British Isles, Costa Rica, Eastern Europe, Turkey, Italy, Greece, Spain, Portugal, or Morocco.

Its traditional Escorted Tours take you to destinations all over the world on international or domestic trips as well as cruises and cruise tours.

Other kinds of adventures offered by Grand Circle Travel include its Discovery series and Elder Venture. On a Discovery trip, you travel to other parts of the world and engage in dialogues with people knowledgeable in the history, art, nature, culture, and politics of the country you are visiting. On Elder Ventures, which are designed to provide close encounters with nature, you have a choice of trips to the Amazon, Belize, Costa Rica, or the Galapagos Islands, where you learn about the ecology, wildlife, geology, and culture of the area.

Single travelers with GCT pay only half of the single supplements on most trips when they have requested a travel roommate and none is available. And on a few Live Abroad departure dates, they pay no supplements at all.

For information: Grand Circle Travel, 347 Congress St., Boston, MA 02210; 800-248-3737 or 617-350-7500.

SAGA HOLIDAYS

Founded in England almost 40 years ago, Saga specializes in travel for people in their prime, targeting travelers over the age of 50. It offers a wide variety of vacations from fully escorted coach tours everywhere in the world to cruises and safaris, educational tours, and winter apartment stays.

Land tours include 32-night grand tours of Europe, cruise-and-coach tours of Greece, holidays in Turkey, and any other place on earth you have ever wanted to go. Cruises range from the coast of Alaska to the waters off China and Vietnam. Saga's Extended Stay Holidays are designed to let you live a while in just one place—such as Portugal, Spain, or England—where you settle into your own furnished apartment or hotel for as many weeks as you like.

Other Saga programs include two educational/travel tours. In partnership with the famous Smithsonian Institution, it offers its own departures of the Smithsonian Odyssey Tours, where you explore the world and learn as you go.

Saga's own Road Scholar program offers travel/study itineraries, each of which features a special educational theme. They include, for example, a 15-night safari in Kenya that's designed to give you an in-depth look at the country, people, and wildlife and a 12-night program in England that concentrates on the great English mystery writers, some of whom serve as lecturers.

For information: Saga Holidays, 222 Berkeley St., Boston, MA 02116; 800-343-0273.

MORE, MORE, MORE

ADRIATIC TOURS
All-inclusive senior tours, relaxed and leisurely, are the specialty of Adriatic Tours, which plans moderate-cost holidays in cities or resorts in Italy, Greece, Croatia, Hungary, and Spain. The trips are planned in one-week modules, and you may add on as many segments as you like.

For information: Adriatic Tours, 691 W. 10th St., San Pedro, CA 90731; 800-262-1718.

AMERICAN JEWISH CONGRESS
AJC sponsors trips all over the world—from China to the British Isles to Scandinavia, Morocco, Egypt, Greece, and Australia—but specializes in heritage expeditions to "The Old Country" (Lithuania, Ukraine, Poland, Czech Republic, Hungary) and tours of Israel, all of which tend to attract mature travelers. Its 15-day

"Israel Slow & Easy" tours are designed for older travelers who want a leisurely pace.

For information: American Jewish Congress, 15 E. 84th St., New York, NY 10028; 800-221-4694 or 212-879-4588, 516-752-1186, or 914-328-0018.

BACK-ROADS TOURING CO.

Designed especially for adults over 50, the tours planned by this agency take small groups (no more than 12 at a time) through the British Isles, Ireland, France, Spain, or Portugal along the back roads to out-of-the-way places. You travel by minivan with a guide for one or two weeks, stay in inns, historic houses, farms, and bed-and-breakfasts, and don't spend a fortune. These are leisurely tours with plenty of time to explore. You may even help plan the itinerary if there are special places you'd like to see. Add-on stays in London are available too. What's more, if you mention this book you will get a discount.

For information: Back-Roads Touring Co., British Network Ltd., 594 Valley Rd., Upper Montclair, NJ 07043; 800-274-8583 or 201-744-5215.

CANADIAN MOTOR COACH TRAVEL

On CMCT's Seniors Travel Together tours, you'll leave from Edmonton, Alberta, and set forth on explorations of Canada and/or the U.S. by luxury motorcoach. Paced especially for mature sightseers, with many stops along the way if only for coffee breaks, the trips may last anywhere from 2 to 21 days.

For information: Canadian Motor Coach Travel Ltd.,

Box 1117, P130 Westmount Shopping Center, Edmonton, AB T5M 3L7; 403-448-1188.

CHOOSING A PLACE TO RETIRE

Lifestyle Explorations conducts two-week group tours in countries that it considers to be ideal retirement destinations. You may choose tours of Costa Rica, Portugal, Uruguay and Argentina, Honduras, Ireland, Canada's Maritime Provinces, or—soon to come—Venezuela and Hungary, combining a vacation with on-site seminars with local professionals and Americans already living there. You'll discover firsthand what it's like to settle there before you make any big decisions. Each area is rated according to cost of living, taxes, health care, climate, safety, friendliness, government stability, and cultural opportunities.

For information: Lifestyle Explorations, 101 Federal St., Ste. 1900, Boston, MA 02110; 508-371-4814.

CORLISS TOURS

The Stay-Put Tours by Corliss are planned with older travelers in mind—you fly to your destination, check into your hotel, and stay put, never packing your bags again until it's time to go home. Meanwhile, you make day trips by motorcoach into the nearby areas, exploring the region in depth. Each tour carries along a tour director who makes all the arrangements and shepherds the group around. Plenty of time, too, to relax and explore on your own. Destinations include Atlanta, Orlando, Washington, D.C., New York, Philadelphia, San Antonio, Seattle, Colorado Springs, Nashville, New Orleans, Montreal, Toronto, Calgary, and Vancouver. Each tour lasts a week, but you may link two or more trips as you like. This agency also specializes in tours, many of them Stay-Puts, over the Thanksgiving and Christmas holidays, taking you to resorts, festivals, and popular vacation destinations.

For information: Corliss Tours, 436 W. Foothill Blvd., Monrovia, CA 91016; 800-456-5717.

ELDERTREKS

Not designed for those who prefer to view the world through bus windows or who will sleep only in five-star hotels, ElderTreks is a program of off-the-beaten-track trips for people 50 and older (and younger companions) who are in reasonably good physical condition, capable of walking at a comfortable pace in tropical conditions. Featuring exotic adventure to relatively remote places in the world, it stresses cultural interaction, physical activity, and nature exploration. However, trekking routes are chosen with older hikers in mind and groups are limited to 15. Trekking portions of the trips are optional and you may choose to substitute a guesthouse-based itinerary.

Accommodations for the city portions of the tours are in clean, comfortable tourist-class hotels and guesthouses. Accommodations on the adventure portions may be on the floor of a house in a tribal village or camping under a canopy of trees in the jungle, but you can always count on having an air mattress to sleep on. Guides, cooks, and porters are part of the package. Destinations include Thailand, Borneo, Vietnam, Costa Rica, Ecuador and the Galapagos Islands, Sumatra, Java and Bali,

Belize, China and Tibet, Nepal, India, and Irian Jaya (New Guinea).
For information: ElderTreks, 597 Markham St., Toronto, ON M6G 2L7; 800-741-7956 or 416-588-5000.

GOLDEN ESCAPES
Golden Escapes for the 50-Plus Traveller are tours run by a Canadian agency that offers all-inclusive escorted tours in Canada, the United States, Great Britain, and on the Continent. In addition, this operator plans lake resort and seaside holidays, cruises, sightseeing adventures in places such as Washington, D.C.; Colonial Williamsburg; and Britain's Channel Islands.
For information: I'm Proud To Be Me Travel Inc., 75 The Donway West, Ste. 910, Don Mills, ON M3C 2E9; 1-800-668-9125 or 416-447-7683.

IDYLL, LTD.
The nontraditional "untours" of Europe planned by Idyll fly you to the country of your choice, escort you to your own private apartment where you'll stay for two or three weeks (or more), provide you with guidance along the way, and map out suggested itineraries for explorations of the countryside on your own. The idea is to provide a home abroad, usually an apartment in a private home, and opportunities to spend time with local people. Round-trip air and ground transportation in the form of rail passes or rental cars is included.
For information: Idyll, Ltd., PO Box 405, Media, PA 19063; 610-565-5242.

MAYFLOWER TOURS

Many of Mayflower's travelers are "55 or better," so the pace of its tours is leisurely and rest stops are scheduled every couple of hours. You travel by motorcoach, stay in good hotels or motels, and eat many of your meals together. All trips are fully escorted by tour directors who make sure all goes well. If you are a single traveler and request a roommate at least 30 days before departure, you'll get a roommate or a room to yourself at the regular double rate. Tours go almost everywhere in the United States and Canada, including national parks of the Southwest, the Canadian Rockies and Pacific Northwest, French Canada, Branson Music and the Ozarks, New England and Cape Cod, Hawaii and New York.
For information: Mayflower Tours, 1225 Warren Ave., Downers Grove, IL 60515; 800-323-7604 or 708-960-3793.

SCRAM TOURS

Senior Citizens Roaming Around the Map, or SCRAM, is a nonprofit agency out of Oregon that plans affordable tours, most of them in the West, for mature travelers and their families. Run by volunteers, its best-known adventure is an 11-day, 2,000-mile motorcoach tour along the Oregon Trail from Missouri to Oregon City, complete with cookouts, gold panning, and a ride on a trail wagon. Other trips include tours in Oregon, California, Nevada, Arizona, Hawaii, the national parks, New Orleans, Vancouver, the Ozarks, and just about any other place you can think of.

For information: SCRAM Travel, 216 SE Emigrant, PO Box 1602, Pendleton, OR 97801; 800-247-2060 (in Oregon, 800-824-5265; in western Canada, 800-426-8348).

SCI/NATIONAL RETIREES OF AMERICA

This agency, which began decades ago with trips to the Catskills resorts, now offers a long list of group tours for seniors that range from one-day outings to 45-day cruises. The land tours—five-day jaunts by air to Las Vegas are its specialty—depart midweek, transport you by motorcoach, and take you to such places as New Orleans, Quebec, Niagara Falls, the Poconos, Orlando, Nashville, or New York.

For information: SCI/National Retirees of America, 343 Merrick Ave., East Meadow, NY 11554; 800-427-7062 or 516-481-3939.

VALUE WORLD TOURS

On certain Value World Tours trips to central and eastern Europe, anybody over the age of 50 gets 10 percent off the regular price. The hosted or escorted tours transport you to a choice of destinations that include Russia, Ukraine, Estonia, Latvia, Lithuania, Poland, Hungary, Czech Republic, Romania, Bulgaria, Turkey, and more. Also available are river cruises in Russia and Ukraine with stops at ports of call along the way.

For information: Value World Tours, 17220 Newhope St., Fountain Valley, CA 92708; 800-795-1633 or 714-556-8258.

SETTLING DOWN IN MEXICO

Retire in Mexico (RIM), a travel company based in California, presents a series of seminars and educational tours for people who are contemplating retirement in Mexico, a neighboring country where the American dollar currently goes very far. Could Mexico provide a happy home for you? You can find out by signing on for a group visit to one or more of about a dozen south-of-the-border areas. You travel around the town and countryside by car or van with a small number of other potential retirees, and attend lectures on such subjects as health facilities, housing, investments, Mexican culture, and immigration.

On a typical tour, for example, you would spend three nights in Mexico City, then two each in San Miguel de Allende, Guanajuato, Morelia, and three in Guadalajara. There are other choices as well, all places with significant populations from north of the border. In each area, you get conferences and tours conducted in English.

For information: Barvi Tours, 11658 Gateway Blvd., Los Angeles, CA 90064; 800-824-7102 or 310-475-1861.

VISTA TOURS

Another agency providing escorted tours almost exclusively for the mature set, Vista Tours plans leisurely trips with plenty of stops and ample time to enjoy the points of interest and relax too. You travel on comfortable motorcoaches with escorts who deal with the reservations, transfers, luggage, meal arrangements, and all other potentially problematic situations. Trips include airfare, lectures, entertainment, and side tours. Destinations, although mainly in the U.S., also include Canada, France, the Far East, Australia, and New Zealand. A

highlight every year is a trip to the Rose Parade in California.
For information: Vista Tours, 1923 N. Carson St., Ste. 105, Carson City, NV 89701; 800-647-0800.

CRUISING THE HIGH SEAS

Cruises have always appealed to the mature crowd. In fact, most sailings abound with people who are at least a few decades out of college. So, whatever trip you choose, you are sure to find suitable companionship. However, there are some special deals designed especially for you.

BERGEN LINE
The cruises in Scandinavia of Color Line, Silja Line, and Norwegian Coastal Voyages, all exclusively represented in North America by Bergen Line, offer special discounts to older travelers. Color Line, Norway's largest cruise passenger company that cruises the North Sea and travels to England and the Continent, gives travelers over 60 and a companion half-price fares on many of its trips. Silja Line, with vessels serving Finland, Sweden, Estonia, and Germany, gives passengers over 65 the same reduced fares it offers teenagers. And Norwegian Coastal Voyages, with ships that take you along the Norwegian coast from Bergen to Kirkenes, north of the Arctic Circle, takes $100 per person off the round-trip fares for seniors over the age of 67 (except in June and July).
For information: Bergen Line, 405 Park Ave., New York, NY 10025; 800-323-7436 or 212-319-1300.

FANTASY CRUISES

If you are 65 or older, you may sign up for a Senior Saver cruise and take a companion along for half price. In other words, a pair of passengers sharing a cabin will end up with a 25 percent reduction off the full fare. You may choose from among several departures from San Juan on the *Amerikanis* and also from Miami on the *Britanis*, seven-night Caribbean cruises, or seven-night cruises along the Mexican coast.

For information: Fantasy Cruises, 800-423-2100.

CRUISE ESCORTS WANTED

Because single men of a certain age are mighty scarce among the traveling population, especially on board ship, a growing number of cruise lines offer free travel or inexpensive travel to carefully chosen unattached men over 50—in one case, over 65—who meet rigorous criteria. These unpaid hosts—usually retired professionals—encourage mingling among the passengers, serve as dancing or dining partners, make a fourth for bridge, act as escorts for shore trips, and generally socialize—without favoritism or romantic entanglements, we are assured—with the single women on board.

There are always many more applicants than positions for them, so don't be surprised if you are not encouraged to apply.

Royal Cruise Line has a roster of screened 50-plus men to act as unofficial hosts on its cruise ships. With four to eight hosts aboard each ship, these congenial fellows spend their evenings whirling around the dance floor, doing their best to see that solo women travelers have a good time.

For information: Host Program, Royal Cruise Line, 1 Maritime Plaza, Ste. 1400, San Francisco, CA 94111.

The **Delta Queen Steamboat Co.**, which makes about 50 cruises a year up and down the Mississippi River, taking you back in time aboard huge paddlewheelers, recruits mature and responsible hosts, assigning two to each trip on the *Mississippi Queen* and four on Big Band cruises to dance every evening with the single women aboard and help them enjoy their voyage. **For information:** Working Vacation, 4277 Santa Clara Dr., Santa Clara, CA 95054.

Sun Lines takes several professional hosts on all of its cruises aboard the *Stella Solaris*. Their assignment is to dance with all the women who love to dance but haven't brought partners with them. **For information:** Host Program, Sun Line Cruises, 1 Rockefeller Plaza, New York, NY 10020.

Regency Cruises takes male hosts along on all of its cruises that are longer than seven days, asking them to circulate among the guests and see that everyone has a good trip. Mostly retired professionals who have been selectively chosen, the hosts act as hospitality directors. **For information:** Working Vacation, 4277 Santa Clara Dr., Santa Clara, CA 95054.

Cunard's cruises aboard *Queen Elizabeth 2*, the *Vistafjord*, the *Sagafjord*, and the *Royal Viking Sun* carry along four to ten friendly gentlemen hosts between the ages of 45 and 70. Their job is not only to whirl around the dance floor with women who need partners but to act as friendly diplomats who help passengers get to know one another. A knowledge of foreign languages is a plus. **For information:** Working Vacation, 4277 Santa Clara Dr., Santa Clara, CA 95054.

Merry Widows Dance Cruises, out of Tampa, offers cruises and tours for single, widowed, or divorced women who were born to dance. Accompanying them are gentlemen hosts (one for every five women) to serve as dance partners.

For information: Merry Widows Dance Tours, 1515 N. Westshore Blvd., Tampa, FL 33607; 800-374-2689.

Crystal Cruises, whose worldwide cruises aboard the *Crystal Harmony* carry four hosts per trip, look for personable social hosts over the age of 65 who are great dancers and enjoy keeping older single women passengers entertained both on board ship and during shore excursions.

For information: Entertainment Dept., Crystal Cruises, 2121 Avenue of the Stars, Los Angeles, CA 90067.

Holland America Line recruits retired professionals with good social skills to act as hosts on its "grand voyages," a world cruise, and a two-month voyage to Australia and New Zealand. Usually four hosts go along on each trip.

For information: Entertainment Dept., Holland America Line, 300 Elliott Ave. West, Seattle, WA 98119.

PREMIER CRUISE LINES

You'll get a discount of 10 to 20 percent, depending on the season, on all of The Big Red Boats visiting Nassau, Port Lucaya, Key West, and Cozumel if you are over 60, and so will a traveling companion who shares your cabin. The discount also applies to The Big Red Boat's seven-night packages that combine cruises with central Florida theme park vacations. Choose from a variety of packages that may include Magic Kingdom Park, EP-COT Center, Sea World, Spaceport USA, and other attractions as well as roundtrip airfare and a rental car with unlimited mileage.

For information: The Big Red Boat, PO Box 573, Cape Canaveral, FL 32920; 800-473-3262.

DANCE CRUISES

Designed for women from 50 to 90 who love to dance but don't have partners, the Merry Widows Dance Tours runs many cruises every year to such places as the Caribbean, the Orient, Alaska, Greece and the Mediterranean, and the South Pacific. The trips range from seven days to 18. Sponsored by the AAA Auto Club South, the cruises take aboard one male professional dancer for every five women. Each woman receives a dance card that rotates her partners every night throughout the cruise, whether she's a beginner or a polished dancer. The men are also rotated at the dinner tables so everyone gets the pleasure of their (platonic) company. You don't have to be a widow and you don't even have to know the cha-cha to have fun on these trips.

Merry Widows also operates tours at a number of major resorts, in such settings as the Cloister in the Georgia Sea Islands, Los Abrigados in Sedona, Arizona, and Sanibel Harbor Spa Resort in Florida. Out-of-the-country destinations include the Greek Isles and Turkey, Mombasa and the Seychelles, Montreal and Nova Scotia, and the Caribbean.

For information: Call your travel agent or contact Merry Widows Dance Tours, 1515 N. Westshore Blvd., Tampa, FL 33607; 800-374-2689.

SINGLEWORLD

Singleworld caters to unattached people who like to travel with other singles and enjoy one another's company. Its trips are segregated according to three age groups: 20s and 30s, "all ages," and Plus 50, which means you. Using major cruise lines, it schedules trips all year with the best bargains to be found off-peak, usually fall or early winter. At this writing, destinations include Caribbean ports, the Bahamas, Mexico, Alaska, Hawaii, Israel, Turkey, and the Mediterranean, among others.

Cruise passengers are guaranteed the second sitting at meals, dining with other singles, exclusive shore excursions, and parties. A cruise director goes along on every voyage to organize shipboard activities and excursions and, in general, to make sure all goes well. Accommodations for solo travelers are arranged on a shared basis, meaning you will be assigned a suitable roommate if you haven't brought your own, and you pay no single supplement.

Singleworld also offers land tours for its solo clientele. Currently, the Plus 50 group has a choice of safaris in Kenya or South Africa; trips to Malaysia, Thailand, and Singapore; a tour of Italy; and a week at a Western dude ranch.

There is a $25 fee to become a Singleworld member and to participate in its trips and receive a quarterly newsletter.

For information: Singleworld, PO Box 1999, Rye, NY 10580; 800-223-6490 or 914-967-3334.

Chapter Six
Singles on the Road

L ots of people over 50 love to travel but don't have anybody to do it with. If you're single, single once again, or have a spouse who isn't the traveling kind, there's no need to give up your dreams of faraway places simply because you don't want to travel alone. There are many organizations and packagers ready to come to your aid. Some offer special trips for mature singles where you mingle with others on their own, and some help match you up with a fellow traveler—of the same or opposite sex—who is also looking for a compatible person with whom to share adventures, a room, and expenses. Traveling with another person is usually more fun and certainly less expensive than going alone because you share double accommodations, thereby avoiding the single supplement which can be substantial.

MATCHMAKERS

TRAVEL COMPANION EXCHANGE
TCE specializes in matching up single travelers so they may go on joint adventures together and always have roommates to share expenses and experiences. Run by travel expert Jens Jurgen, who works very hard at making compatible connections, TCE is the largest, most enduring, and most successful matchmaking service.

Members receive bulky bimonthly newsletters packed with travel tips and helpful advice plus long listings of people (TCE now has close to 3,000 active members) who are seeking new friends and/or travel partners. For more information about those who seem to be good possibilities, you send for Profile Pages about them (meanwhile, others send for yours) so you may judge their suitability for yourself. You do your own matchmaking. Jurgen suggests you talk by telephone, correspond, meet, and, even better, take a short trip together before setting out on a major adventure.

Currently, you may join TCE at a half-price introductory fee of $66 for six months or $120 for a year if you mention this book. Credit cards are accepted. By the way, you may subscribe to the *Newsletter for Solo Travelers* alone (without listings) for $39 per year. It is a gold mine of useful, up-to-the-minute travel information.

For information: Travel Companion Exchange Inc., PO Box 833, Amityville, NY 11701; 800-392-1256 or 516-454-0880. Send $5 for a sample newsletter.

GOLDEN COMPANIONS

Exclusively for travelers over 45, Golden Companions specializes in finding travel companions for the mature set. It is a network of solo travelers in the U.S. and Canada who are looking for others to join them on their journeys, providing them with friends, safety, and shared expenses. To become a member, you complete a form describing your personal and travel interests and the travel mate you are seeking. Brief descriptions of members are included in a directory, identified only by code numbers. To contact others, you write to them through a free mail exchange service and do your own matchmaking. Travel discounts and get-togethers are included, as is an informative bimonthly newsletter, *Golden Gateways*. The newsletter is also offered to non-members by subscription. Annual dues are $85.

For information: Golden Companions, PO Box 754, Pullman, WA 99163; 208-858-2183. Send $2 if you'd like a sample newsletter.

PARTNERS FOR TRAVEL

Partners for Travel, a matchmaking service for singles over the age of 50, introduces you to prospective traveling companions by sending you miniprofiles of all of its several hundred members. From these, you select those you'd like to know more about and, finally, talk or write to them before settling on one to accompany you on your next trip. A yearly membership costs $60 and includes a newsletter, news bulletins, and regional social gatherings. The annual signature event is Singlefest, where single, divorced, and widowed men and women get together from all parts of the country for a week of social networking.

Another program is a series of educational adventure trips and cruises open to any traveler over 50, member or not.

For information: Partners for Travel, PO Box 560337, Miami, FL 33256-0337; 800-866-5565.

PARTNERS-IN-TRAVEL

This group is devoted to making travel a happy experience for solo voyagers through contacts and connections.

Sign on for its Super-Saver package (membership fee is $25) and you will receive a directory of singles mainly on the West Coast, who want to link up with travel companions, a listing of tour operators that package singles tours or arrange shares, and other handy brochures. An alternative is to join the network without charge and, after completing a questionnaire, have your name and preferences listed in the next directory.

For information: Partners-in-Travel, 11660 Chenault St., Ste. 119, Los Angeles, CA 90049; 310-476-4869.

SAGA HOLIDAYS

Join the Saga Club ($49.95 per year) and you may participate in Penfriends & Partnerships, a way to strike up a correspondence with other travelers around the country and perhaps find a travel companion to share trips. You send an entry about yourself and the person you are seeking, or you respond to somebody else's notice in *Saga Magazine*, the club's quarterly newsletter. Club members also get tips on last-minute travel specials, discounts, shipboard credits, and upgrades.

For information: Saga Holidays, 222 Berkeley St., Boston, MA 02116; 800-343-0273.

TOURS FOR SOLO TRAVELERS

Several tour operators and agencies specializing in escorted trips for people in their prime will try to find you a roommate (of the same sex) to share your room or cabin so you will not have to pay a supplement. And, if they can't manage to find a suitable roommate, they will usually reduce the supplement even though you'll have your own private room. Some run singles trips as well. In any case, keep in mind that you'll hardly have time or opportunity to be lonely on the typical escorted tour run by these agencies. If you are planning an extended stay in one location, however, you may have more need for company.

For more about the tour operators listed below, see Chapter 5. Other companies may offer the same singles-matching service, though they don't make a point of it, so always ask about it if you're interested.

BALLROOM DANCERS WITHOUT PARTNERS
This agency specializes in cruises for men and women who are suddenly single, like to travel, and love to dance. No need to take a partner along because dance hosts see to it that you never lack for attention. You'll have a choice of cruises to the Caribbean or Mexico.
For information: Ballroom Dancers Without Partners, 1449 NW 15th St., Miami, FL 33125; 407-361-9384.

GOLDEN AGE TRAVELLERS
An over-50 club, Golden Age Travellers will enroll you in its "Roommates Wanted" list if you wish help in finding a companion with whom to share the costs and the fun. See Chapter 5 for more information about this club.
For information: Golden Age Travellers, Pier 27, The Embarcadero, San Francisco, CA 94111; 800-258-8880.

GRAND CIRCLE TRAVEL
Grand Circle, which concentrates on over-50 travel packages, tries to match singles with appropriate roommates

if they request them. If there are none at hand, you will be charged only half the single supplement for your own room on most trips. And on several of its Live Abroad Vacations departure dates, you will not pay the single supplement at all. See Chapter 5 for more about Grand Circle.

For information: Grand Circle Travel, 347 Congress St., Boston, MA 02210; 800-248-3737.

MATURE TOURS

Mature Tours, a division of Solo Flights, specializes in travel for over-50s who want to travel with other single people their own age, avoiding the trips that attract the 25-year-olds on the one hand and the nonadventurous golden agers on the other. Current trips include a steamboat cruise out of New Orleans, a show tour of London over New Year's, and a week in Costa Rica.

For information: Mature Tours, 612 Penfield Rd., Fairfield, CT 06430; 800-266-1566 or 203-256-1235.

MAYFLOWER TOURS

Another travel operator with mature travelers as its focus, Mayflower will also get you a roommate if you like or, if that's not possible, absorb the cost of the single-room supplement. You'll then pay the regular twin rate.

For information: Mayflower Tours, 1225 Warren Ave., Downers Grove, IL 60515; 800-323-7604 or 708-960-3430.

MERRY WIDOWS DANCE TOURS

If you are a single woman over 50 who was born to dance, consider a trip with the Merry Widows. Known

for its cruises, it also has land tours that transport you to exciting places on this continent and abroad, not only to dance but also to see the sights. If you're traveling alone, you'll be assigned a roommate if you want one. See Chapter 5 for more.
For information: Merry Widows Dance Tours, 1515 N. Westshore Blvd., Tampa, FL 33607; 800-374-2689.

SAGA HOLIDAYS
A tour company specializing in trips for people over 50, Saga Holidays will try to find a roommate for you on its escorted tours and cruises so you won't have to pay the single supplement. And on some of its vacations, it doesn't charge a single supplement at all. See Chapter 5.
For information: Saga Holidays, 222 Berkeley St., Boston, MA 02116; 800-343-0273.

SINGLETOURS
If you don't want to be a single traveler on a tour filled with couples, Singletours has the answer for you. It offers a series of motorcoach trips expressly for single travelers 45 and up. The tours to foreign lands are first class, fully escorted, and leisurely paced, mostly with stays of two or three nights so you needn't spend your time packing and unpacking your bags. What's more, you may have a single or a double room, and if you request a roommate to share your accommodations but none is available, you will travel as a single at no extra charge. The current offerings include 12- to 16-day tours in England, Switzerland, France, Scandinavia, Spain, and Italy.
For information: Singletours by Uniworld Global, 16000 Ventura Blvd., Encino, CA 91436; 800-733-7820.

SINGLEWORLD

To help you enjoy vacationing in the company of others while avoiding single-supplement fees, Singleworld offers its members cruises and land tours specifically for solo travelers (see Chapter 5). Members, who pay a membership fee of $25 a year, also receive a quarterly newsletter. Sign up for one of Singleworld's Plus 50 departures.

For information: Singleworld, PO Box 1999, Rye, NY 10580; 800-223-6490 or 914-967-3334.

A WEEK IN THE SUN

Club Med's Forever Young program offers travelers 55 and over a discount of $150 on weeklong vacations at six of its villages that it deems especially suited to them: Caravelle, in Guadaloupe; Paradise Island, in Nassau; Ixtapa, in Mexico; Sandpiper, in Florida; Eleuthera, in the Bahamas; and Cancun, in Mexico. The program is year-round (except for major holidays) and promises good shopping, interesting excursions, golf courses, sports, no hills, and little stair climbing.

For information: Call your travel agent or 800-CLUB MED.

SOLO FLIGHTS

This travel agency specializes in vacations for single travelers of all ages, with much of its clientele on the far side of 50. It makes it its business to know about the best tours, cruises, packages, groups, and rates for unpartnered people, and so, with one telephone call or a letter, you can find out—at no charge—what's out there that interests you. Its suggestions range from cruises to European tours offered by major tour operators specifically for singles. Recent possibilities have included walking tours in England, Windjammer singles cruises, Club Med, and packages to Costa Rica, Europe, and the American Southwest. In return for its services, the agency does your booking.

For information: Solo Flights, 612 Penfield Rd., Fairfield, CT 06430; 800-266-1566 or 203-256-1235.

HOOK-UPS FOR LONE RVers

RVers who travel alone in their motor homes or vans can hook up with others in the same circumstances when they join one of the groups mentioned below. All of the clubs provide opportunities to travel together or to meet at campgrounds on the road, making friends with fellow travelers, and having fun.

LONERS OF AMERICA

LOA is a club for single RVers who want to travel together. In existence only since 1988, it now has 29 chapters throughout the country and 1,400 members from their 40s to their 90s, almost all retired and all widowed, divorced, or otherwise single. Many of them live year-round in their motor homes or vans, and others hit the road only occasionally. They camp together, rally together, caravan together, often meeting at special campgrounds that cater to solo RVers.

A not-for-profit member-operated organization, the club sends you an annual membership directory and a lively bimonthly newsletter that alerts you to campouts and rallies all over the country. The chapters organize their own events as well. Currently, dues are $23 a year plus a $5 registration fee for new members.

For information: Loners of America, Rte. 2, Box 85E, Ellsinore, MO 63937; 314-322-5548.

THE FRIENDLY ROAMERS

Founded by former members of Loners on Wheels, a club for singles traveling alone, The Friendly Roamers was organized for people who—because of a change in marital status or travel arrangements—no longer qualify for LOW. Open to all RVers, singles or couples, its members are all over 50 and most of them are retired. Members participate in hosting campouts and sharing their talents with other members. Membership (currently, dues are $15 for the first year and $10 a year thereafter) entitles you to all events, a quarterly newsletter, a membership directory, caravans, campouts, and rallies. You may also choose to join one of five regional chapters.

For information: The Friendly Roamers, c/o Joyce Keagle, 112 Whittier Ave., Ben Lomond, CA 95005; 408-336-8203.

LONERS ON WHEELS

A camping and travel club for mature single campers, Loners on Wheels is not a lonely hearts club or a matchmaking service, but simply an association of friends and extended family. With about 60 chapters located throughout the United States and Canada, it now has a membership of about 2,800 single travelers. The club schedules hundreds of camping events during the year, at sites that are usually remote and/or primitive and

cost little. A monthly newsletter and an annual directory keep everyone up to date and in touch. Annual dues
at this writing are $36 U.S. and $45 Canada.
For information (and a free sample newsletter): Loners
on Wheels, PO Box 1355, Poplar Bluff, MO 63902.

RVing WOMEN

A club for women who travel in recreational vehicles,
RVing Women was designed to be a support group for
women alone on the road. It provides a forum through
which they can make contacts and travel connections
with other women on their own, perhaps linking up to
travel and caravan together. For a $39 annual member-
ship fee, members receive a bimonthly newsletter full of
technical and travel information, a directory of members (many of whom encourage overnight stays with
information on hookups and assistance), and a free U.S.
trip-routing service. More than 50 regional rallies are
scheduled every year all over the U.S., and caravans,
limited to 10 rigs each, move out together every so often
for weeklong trips throughout Alaska, Canada, and
Mexico. A resident resort park also has been established
in Arizona for members only.
For information: RVing Women, 201 E. Southern Ave.,
Apache Junction, AZ 85219; 602-982-7247.

Chapter Seven
Airfares:
Improving with Age

One thing that improves with age—yours—is air-fare. Almost every airline now offers senior coupon books that are among the outstanding buys in today's marketplace. The basic idea is simple: If you are 62 or over, you may buy the coupons, each good for a one-way trip within the lower 48 states and sometimes beyond. On long flights, they can save you a good deal of money. And almost every airline—both domestic and foreign—also gives senior travelers and a traveling companion of any age a 10 percent discount off the regular fares. Other ways of attracting mellow travelers include clubs that give you discounts and other privileges, and senior passes that allow you virtually unlimited travel for a year at a flat rate.

You get these nice offers because you, the mature population, have proved to be the hottest travel market around, a vast and growing group of careful consumers with money in your pockets and time on your hands midweek and during the slack off-peak travel periods, just when the airlines are eager to fill up seats.

Several airlines have arrangements with car-rental companies and hotel chains to provide discounts on these, too. (See Chapter 8 for more on car rentals and Chapter 10 for more on hotels and motels.)

But, first, keep in mind:

▶ Always ask your travel agent or the airline reservations clerk to get you the *lowest possible fare*. Mention the fact that you qualify for a senior discount, but be prepared to jump ship if you can get a better deal by going with a special promotional rate or a supersaver fare—although sometimes your discount can cut these low fares even lower. Most airlines now offer promotional fares during off-peak seasons, sometimes specifically for seniors. Watch for these sales because they are usually the cheapest way to go, although in most cases you can't deduct the regular senior discount from them.

▶ Keep in mind that the restrictions you must fly by may not be worth the savings. Always examine the fees and conditions and decide whether you can live with them. There may be blackout periods around major holidays when you can't use your privileges, departures only on certain days or hours, restrictions on the season of the year, or stiff penalties for flight changes. In some plans, you must travel the entire distance on one airline even if connections are poor. It's not always easy to sort out the offers.

▶ Before you decide to buy a yearly pass, figure out how many trips you're likely to make during the next year. Unless you see clear savings, you are better off with individual tickets or coupon books. But if you travel frequently, or would do so once you had the pass, then it could be an excellent buy.

▶ A 10 percent senior discount is obviously better than nothing, but on all but short trips you'll probably do much better with a coupon book if you fly often enough.

▶ Try to couple your senior discount with ultimate supersaver fares, which require 30-day advance purchase and include other restrictions.

▶ Be prepared to present valid proof of age at the check-in counter. It's possible that your discount will not be honored if you don't have that proof with you, and you will have to pay the difference.

▶ Eight-coupon books cost less per flight than four-coupon books. Coupon travel earns frequent-flyer credit on all of the domestic airlines. Reservations must usually be made 14 days in advance, although most airlines allow you to use the coupons for standby travel. Once issued, the coupons must be traded in for tickets within a year, although you may fly at a later date.

Always watch for special promotional fares that may be better than your coupon rate, checking for the lowest available fare. Using your coupons may not be a bargain when airline wars are going on and fares are slashed.

Don't waste coupons on short hops. The longer the distance, the greater your savings off regular fares. For long hauls, the cost of a round trip can be just about half what you'd pay otherwise, but using coupons for short trips usually doesn't pay.

▶ Book your flights as early as possible for the best fares and the most available seats. As with most tickets sold at deep discounts, only a limited number of coupon holders can be accommodated on a single flight.

▶ Be flexible. To get the best fares when you use your senior discount, plan to fly at off-peak times, when the rest of the population isn't rushing off to faraway places. For example, check the fares at different times of day. Noontime or late-night flights can be much cheaper than early-morning or dinnertime flights. Consider leaving on a different day. Often fares are lower midweek or on Saturday. And obviously, flying off-season, when children aren't on vacation and there are no major holidays, pays off with better prices.

Now for some of the potential bargain offers. Be advised that airfares and airline policies can change overnight—and often do—so always call the airline that interests you for an update.

U.S. AIRLINES

ALASKA AIRLINES
Fly on Alaska Airlines at 62-plus and you'll get 10 percent off almost all fares along with frequent-flyer credits. So will a traveling companion of any age.
For information: Call your travel agent or 800-426-0333.

AMERICA WEST
America West currently offers an excellent deal on coast-to-coast senior booklets. Its Senior Saver Pack, for travelers over the age of 62, gives you four one-way flights at discounted prices wherever it flies within the continental U.S., or eight one-way trips for even less per trip. Travel days are limited to noon on Monday through noon on Thursday and all day Saturday. Seats are limited, and reservations must be made 14 days in advance,

although standby is allowed. There are some blackout periods around major holidays.

In addition, America West gives you a discount of 10 percent on regular coach fares. But be sure to ask about the special senior fares offered on some flights—they may be even better deals for you.

For information: Call your travel agent or 800-235-9292.

AMERICAN AIRLINES
American Airlines offers two good deals if you are 62. One is a 10 percent discount on any regular fare, even the lowest, for you and a traveling companion. The other is its Senior TrAAveler Coupon Books, which give you four-coupon or eight-coupon books at good per-trip prices. Traded in for a ticket, each coupon is good for travel one way in the 48 contiguous states as well as Puerto Rico, St. Thomas, and St. Croix. Hawaii requires two coupons each way.

You may travel any day of the week, but you must buy your tickets at least 14 days in advance of your flight. There is no refund on the coupons and no change of itinerary on one-way tickets, although if you don't take your reserved flight, you may use the ticket for a standby seat. On round trips, you may change your outbound flight at least 14 days before the flight for a $25 service charge. You may change your return any time for a $25 service charge. Seats are limited, but you will be entitled to frequent-flyer credits for all the miles you fly. The same privileges apply to flights on American Eagle, AA's commuter airline.

Another program, Senior SAAvers Club, is no longer

open for enrollment, but if you are already a lifetime member, you'll continue to get its newsletter and a 10 percent discount on your fares.

For information: Call your travel agent or 800-433-7300 for reservations. For the Senior TrAAveler Coupon Books, call 800-237-7981.

CONTINENTAL AIRLINES

Continental Airlines has some of the best deals out there for senior travelers and now offers three different options. The first is a 10 percent discount on all fares, even the lowest, if you are 62. Just ask for it and be ready to prove your age. Even with the discount you'll be eligible for frequent flyer points.

Or consider the Freedom Passport, also for people over 62. The domestic passport, available for four months or one year, gives you virtually unlimited travel in the continental U.S., Canada, and the U.S. Virgin Islands. Then, using low-cost options, you may add on trips to Mexico, Central America, Hawaii, Europe, or the Caribbean. The global passport, more expensive, lets you fly all over the world in a year's time. A companion passport for a travel mate may be purchased at the same price. Drawback: No frequent-flyer credits are issued for flights purchased with the passport.

Here are the restrictions on the Freedom Passport: You may fly to the same city only three times during the year. Seats are limited, and there are some periods around major holidays when no passport seats are available. For domestic flights, the general rule is that travel is restricted to noon on Monday through noon on Thursday plus all day Saturday. A Sunday-night stay is required. Reservations may be made no earlier than seven days in advance. For international flights, the general rule is that you must travel Monday through Thursday or on Saturday, and reservations may be made no earlier than 30 days in advance.

A third option offered by Continental is its Freedom Trips. These are booklets of four or eight discounted coupons that may be traded in for tickets on flights anywhere the airline goes within the United States, Mexico, the Caribbean, and Bermuda. Flights to Hawaii, Alaska, Mexico, the Caribbean, and Bermuda will cost you two coupons each way. You must make reservations at least 14 days in advance, though standby is allowed. You may fly any day of the week except for blackout periods around major holidays. You will receive frequent-flyer points for your mileage.

For information: Call your travel agent or 800-525-0280 for reservations, or call 800-441-1135 for the Freedom Passport.

DELTA AIRLINES

If you are 62, Delta takes 10 percent off the regular fares for you and a younger traveling partner for flights between cities in the U.S. and to most of its many overseas destinations. Seats are limited, so book early. You'll be eligible for mileage points when you use the discount.

Another worthwhile option from Delta is its Young at Heart Coupon Program for travelers over 62, which gives you books of four or eight coupons that let you travel at reduced rates if you use them all within a year's time. Each coupon may be traded for a ticket to any Delta or Delta Connection city in the continental

U.S., Puerto Rico, or the U.S. Virgin Islands. Two coupons are required each way for Alaska or Hawaii. You may fly any day of the week but, as with all special fares, seats are limited, so book as far ahead as possible. Reservations or changes must be made at least 14 days before departure, although you may travel standby any time. You will get frequent-flyer credits for the miles you fly.

For information: Call your travel agent or 800-221-1212.

DELTA SHUTTLE

For shuttle flights between New York and Washington, D.C., or Boston, you get the Senior Fare, currently half of the fare for other adults—that is, if you are 62 and can provide evidence of that fact a half hour before flight time. And you are eligible for frequent-flyer credits for your miles. With this fare, you must fly between 10:30 A.M. and 2:30 P.M. or 7:30 P.M. and 9:30 P.M. Monday through Friday or all day Saturday or Sunday. No reservations are required. Just show up at the gate.

A second option is the Senior Flight Pack, four or eight one-way tickets that must be used within a year on flights that leave in off-peak hours: 10:30 A.M. to 2:30 P.M. or 7:30 to 9:30 P.M. Monday through Friday and all day Saturday or Sunday. For this good deal, you must be at least 62. Frequent-flyer credits apply. The Flight Pack may be purchased only in a shuttle city—although you may buy a voucher through your travel agent and trade it for the booklet when you arrive at the airport.

For information: Call your travel agent or 800-221-1212.

HAWAIIAN AIRLINES

At age 60, you and a traveling companion are entitled to a 10 percent discount on any published fare from coach excursion to first class on flights from the mainland to Hawaii, including connecting flights to neighboring islands. If you are flying to Samoa or Tahiti, you (but not a companion) get a 20 percent discount on the regular fare.

For information: Call your travel agent or 800-367-5320.

KIWI INTERNATIONAL AIR LINES

Kiwi, which flies to and from New York (Newark), Chicago, Atlanta, Tampa, Orlando, West Palm Beach, and San Juan, has two programs for travelers 62 and older. The first offers a 10 percent discount on all air tickets, except for some special promotional fares, for you and a traveling companion of any age. Be sure to have a photo ID with you when you check in. Kiwi's fares do not require 7-day, 14-day, or 21-day advance purchases on Saturday stayovers.

The second is a Senior Discount Pack, a coupon book for six one-way tickets that may be used any day of the week and give you substantial savings over the regular costs—depending, of course, on your destination. The nonrefundable coupons, valid for a year after purchase, may not be used for flights to or from San Juan. There are no blackout periods when you cannot use the coupons and no fees for cancellation or changes. Reservations must be made within seven days of departure.

For information: Call your travel agent or 800-538-5494.

MARKAIR

This Alaska-based airline gives passengers over 62 a 10 percent discount on the regular fares. It also sells senior coupon books that can save you money on four or eight flights taken within one year, especially if you use the coupons on coast-to-coast flights. Two coupons are required when you fly to or from Alaska, only one between cities in the lower 48.

For information: Call your travel agent or 800-627-5247.

MIDWEST EXPRESS

Ten percent is the discount on published fares for people over the age of 62 and traveling companions on Midwest Express, an airline that flies out of Milwaukee.

For information: Call your travel agent or 800-452-2022.

NORTHWEST AIRLINES

You'll get a senior discount of 10 percent on Northwest's published fares once you've reached the age of 62. So will your younger travel mate. You will get frequent-flyer mileage as well.

You are also eligible at 62 to buy the airline's North-Best Senior Coupons, with each coupon good for a one-way flight in the continental United States or Canada. Flights to Hawaii, Alaska, or the Caribbean cost two coupons. You must trade in all your coupons within the year. You may fly any time, any day, accruing frequent-flyer miles, but you must make your reservations at least 14 days in advance.

For information: Call your travel agent or 800-225-2525.

SOUTHWEST AIRLINES
This airline, which flies mainly in the southwestern United States, offers special senior fares to travelers over 65 that vary from city to city and change frequently. However, they are guaranteed to match the lowest promotional fare out there, and you get mileage points for your flights. Reservations are required but advance purchase is not necessary. The senior fares are available for every flight every day of the week, but seats are limited. Your tickets, one-way or round-trip, are fully refundable.
For information: Call your travel agent or 800-435-9792.

TWA (TRANSWORLD AIRLINES)
This airline reduces the fare by 10 percent for travelers over 62 and companions of any age on almost all flights in the U.S. and Puerto Rico and some to Europe as well. Ask for the discount when you make your reservations. You'll get frequent-flyer credits for your mileage.

The Senior Travel Pak is another alternative offered by TWA. This gives you four one-way domestic coupons at bargain prices. Each coupon may be exchanged for a one-way ticket on flights in the United States and to Puerto Rico. You also get a 20-percent-off certificate for travel to Europe, two coupons for upgrades on car rentals, and coupons for discounts on TWA land vacations in Europe. Within the lower 48 states, you may fly any day of the week except from 12 noon to 7:00 P.M. on Sundays and during blackouts around major holidays. To Hawaii and San Juan, flying days are limited to Tuesday, Wednesday, or Thursday only. Two coupons each way are required for trips between the mainland and Hawaii, but the coupons may not be exchanged for tickets on flights to Hawaii from June 1 through August 15. Frequent-flyer miles also are yours when you fly on your coupons.

TWA was the first airline to come out with companion coupon books to go along with its senior coupons. If a traveler who is over 62 buys a book of four coupons, a younger person may buy four companion coupons to be used only when they travel together. The companion books cost more than the senior books, but they are still a bargain and include the certificate for Europe at a discount. All four companion coupons must be used by the same person.

You must book passage 14 days in advance, but you may travel standby anytime before your flight once you have traded in your coupon for a ticket. And you'll earn points for your mileage when you use your coupons.
For information: Call your travel agent or 800-221-2000.

UNITED AIRLINES
You may join United's Silver Wings Plus travel club at age 60 and become eligible for many benefits, such as discounts on hotels, rental cars, and special travel packages and cruises. Sign up for a lifetime membership at $225 and you receive three $50 certificates for future travel. Sign up for two years at a cost of $75 and you get three $25 certificates to use within a year. You'll earn Mileage Plus miles and upgrades and will receive the *Silver Wings Plus* newsletter.

Then, when you turn 62, you and a companion who flies with you will be eligible for a 10 percent discount on all published airfares, even discount fares, from United Airlines, United Express, and the Shuttle by United; on selected routes with international partners; and on fares from regional carriers such as British Midland, Ansett Australia Airlines, and Mount Cook Airlines of New Zealand.

United's other good deal for travelers over 62 is the Silver TravelPac program. This gives you packets of four or eight discount coupons that let you fly at lower fares any day of the week when seats are available, although there are some blackout periods. Each coupon is good for a one-way ticket within the lower 48 states and to San Juan. Two coupons are needed each way to Hawaii or Alaska.

You must make your reservations at least 14 days in advance or travel on standby. You will earn Mileage Plus miles when you use the coupons. Just remember, seats at senior fares are limited, so always plan ahead.
For information: Call your travel agent or 800-241-6522 for reservations. Call 800-628-2868 for United Silver Wings Plus; or call 800-633-6563 for the United Silver TravelPac program.

USAir
If you are over 62, you and a fellow traveler are entitled to a 10 percent discount on any fare on USAir flights, so be sure to ask for it when you make your reservations.

In addition, USAir offers its Golden Opportunities Coupon Books. You may buy, at a low per-trip cost, a book of four one-way coupons or, at even less per trip, a book of eight one-way coupons. Each coupon may be traded for a ticket to any destination within the continental United States, Canada, St. Thomas, or Puerto Rico, including flights on affiliated commuter lines. Good for a year, the coupon books may be purchased when you are 62. Reservations must be made at least 14 days in advance, or you may travel standby any time before your booked flight once your ticket has been issued. You may fly any day of the week except for blackout periods around holidays. You'll get mileage points for all the miles you fly.

Bonus: a coupon may also be traded for a ticket for a grandchild age 2 through 11 who flies with you.

For information: Call your travel agent or 800-428-4322.

USAir FLORIDA SHUTTLE

The new Florida Shuttle operates frequent flights between 20 cities in Florida. Seniors age 65 and over get 10 percent off the regular fares. That's good news unless promotional seat sales offer the flights for less.

For information: Call your travel agent or 800-428-4322.

USAir SHUTTLE

If you are over 65, you may fly at half price on this airline's hourly shuttle flights between New York and Boston or Washington, D.C., if you are willing to travel off-peak. You may fly Monday through Friday from 10:00 A.M. to 2:00 P.M. and 7:00 P.M. to 9:00 P.M., as well as all day Saturday or Sunday.

Even more cost effective for mature travelers who fly the shuttle frequently is the Senior FlightPass, which is good for a year's use. This is a book of four or eight

coupons, each of which may be traded for a ticket on a flight that is taking off during the same off-peak hours.
For information: Call your travel agent or 800-428-4322.

VIRGIN ATLANTIC AIRLINES
On all flights from the United States to London, Virgin Atlantic gives you a 10 percent discount on all regular fares as soon as you turn 60. Ask for it when you make your reservations. In addition, the airline frequently offers special promotional fares for seniors that give you a much deeper discount—sometimes as much as 50 percent.
For information: Call your travel agent or 800-862-8621.

GOOD DEALS ON CANADIAN AIRLINES

AIR CANADA
If you are over 60, you and a traveling companion of any age are eligible for a 10 percent reduction on most fares, including special promotions, for flights in Canada and the U.S. At age 62, you will get the same discount on joint flights with Continental Airlines. The markdown also applies to Air Canada trips between Canada and the U.K. and the Caribbean. What's more, you'll get points for your mileage.

Air Canada's Freedom Flyer program is another good choice for travelers over the age of 60 who want to save money on airfares. This plan gives you four or eight one-way tickets at big savings. The same savings apply to your traveling companion. Make your reservations at least two weeks before departure. Frequent-flyer credits are given for these flights too.

For information: Call your travel agent or 800-776-3000.

CANADIAN AIRLINES INTERNATIONAL

This airline has two good options for passengers over 60 and their traveling companions. The first is the Canadian Golden Discount, which gives you a 10 percent reduction on all round-trip fares on Canadian Airlines and its commuter partners to destinations within Canada and the continental U.S. and on certain fares to Hawaii and London. You get frequent-flyer credits for your mileage, and there are no special restrictions on time, day, or season.

The second choice is the 60/60 Discount, which entitles travelers over 60 and their companions to 60 percent off the price of full-fare economy tickets much of the year on flights to most destinations within Canada. This option includes two free stops along the way.

For information: Call your travel agent or 800-426-7000 in the U.S.; 800-665-1177 in Canada.

GOOD DEALS ON FOREIGN AIRLINES

Again, always inquire about special senior discounts when you book a flight, even if you don't see them listed here. Airlines change their policies with very little notice. Your travel agent can provide current information.

AEROLINEAS ARGENTINAS

On this airline, there's an offer of a 10 percent discount for passengers over 60 on posted fares for round-trip flights originating in the United States to South American destinations.

For information: Call your travel agent or 800-333-0276.

AEROLITORAL

A commuter airline operated by Aeromexico that flies from several cities in the U.S. Southwest to Mexico, Aerolitoral offers a 50 percent discount on its regular economy fares to passengers over 62. In this case, you need not be accompanied by a fellow traveler.

For information: Call your travel agent or 800-237-7113.

AEROMEXICO

It's 10 percent off the regular first-class or tourist fares on all Aeromexico routes, domestic and international, if you are over 60 *and* travel with a companion of any age who may also take advantage of the senior discount. There are blackouts for these senior fares, however, during major holidays.

For information: Call your travel agent or 800-237-6639.

AIR FRANCE

A 10 percent discount is yours at age 62 on Air France flights between its major U.S. gateway cities and France. It also applies to a traveling companion who may be younger, and it is deducted from almost every fare including the Concorde. If you are a World War II veteran and have documents to prove it, you can get an even better deal on Air France through 1995. This is a 30 percent discount off most round-trip transatlantic fares for you and up to three accompanying family members, including grandchildren.

For information: Call your travel agent or 800-237-2747.

AIR INTER

The major domestic airline in France, Air Inter gives travelers over the age of 60 some excellent reduced fares on its flights to 31 cities within the country. Usually amounting to 40 to 60 percent off the full fare, the senior tickets are available on almost all flights. Simply show proof of age when you purchase your tickets.

For information: Call your travel agent or 800-237-2747.

ALITALIA

When you fly on Alitalia to its European destinations or Egypt, you qualify for a 10 percent discount when you are 62, as will a younger traveling companion. When you travel via Alitalia from the U.S. to Israel, you will get a 15 percent discount if you are 60. So will your spouse if he or she accompanies you and is at least 55.

On domestic flights within Italy, seniors over 62 are offered special discounted fares. Be sure to ask for them.

For information: Call your travel agent or 800-223-5730.

BRITISH AIRWAYS
The good deal offered by British Airways to travelers over 60 and a companion of any age is a discount of 10 percent on all advance-purchase economy-class airfares, plus a waiver of the usual pretrip cancellation penalties. This applies to travel from 17 U.S. gateway cities to the UK and Europe.

For information: Call your travel agent or 800-247-9297.

BWIA
British West Indies Airlines takes 10 percent off the regular fares for you at 62 and a fellow traveler at any age.

For information: Call your travel agent or 800-327-7401.

EL AL
Travelers over the age of 60 and their spouses over 55 are entitled to El Al's senior fare, which gives you a discount of about 15 percent off the regular Apex fare between the U.S. and Israel. You may stay for up to two months, a 14-day advance purchase is required, and there is a $50 fee for changing your return flight. With your ticket you'll receive a coupon booklet for discounts on merchandise, museums, tourist sites, car rentals, and cultural events.

But, before accepting this deal, check out the cheaper Superapex fare with its maximum stay of 21 days. It may work out better for you.

Traveling with your grandchildren? If they are under

12, the first one flies at 25 percent off, the second at 50 percent off, and the third at 75 percent off.
For information: Call your travel agent or 800-223-6700.

FINNAIR

On flights between New York and Helsinki, Finland, you will get a 10 percent reduction off the regular economy fares if you are 62 years old or more. Travel companions of any age get the same discount.
For information: Call your travel agent or 800-950-5000.

IBERIA

Iberia gives you 10 percent off regular published fares for transatlantic flights, except on special promotions. You must have reached 62 to get the privilege, but you may take a younger companion who pays the same fare.
For information: Call your travel agent or 800-772-4642.

KLM ROYAL DUTCH AIRLINES

KLM's discount for people over the age of 62 is 10 percent on all nonpromotional fares between the U.S. and its European destinations. A companion of any age gets the same reduction in fare if you travel together for the entire journey.
For information: Call your travel agent or 800-777-5553.

LUFTHANSA

At age 60, you can get a 10 percent reduction on most fares, including first-class, business, and economy, for yourself and another adult travel mate, on Lufthansa flights to and from the U.S. and Germany. Seats are limited and you must request the discount when you make your reservations. You will get frequent-flyer mileage points.

For information: Call your travel agent or 800-645-3880.

MEXICANA AIRLINES

A senior discount of 10 percent applies to all Mexicana international flights between gateway cities in the U.S. and Mexico, including stopovers, except in July and August from Los Angeles, San Francisco, and San Juan and in blackout periods around major holidays. You must be 62, but your traveling companion may be younger and get the same rate.

For information: Call your travel agent or 800-531-7921.

SABENA (BELGIAN WORLD AIRLINES)

At 62, you are entitled to a 10 percent discount on almost all fares from the United States to Belgium and via Brussels to other Sabena destinations in Europe. In addition, Sabena offers special discounted senior fares to travelers over 60 on flights to Tel Aviv.

For information: Call your travel agent or 800-950-1000.

SAS (SCANDINAVIAN AIRLINES)

Flying on SAS across the Atlantic Ocean from this continent to Scandinavia will get you a 10 percent reduction in your fare if you are 62 or older. You are also entitled to a 50 percent discount on domestic flights within Sweden and 25 percent on flights within Denmark. In Norway, domestic flights are half price at age 67. Remember to take your passport with you for proof of age when you buy your tickets.

For information: Call your travel agent or 800-221-2350.

SWISSAIR

Swissair offers two good deals to travelers over the age of 62 and their younger traveling companions. One is a 10 percent discount on all regular round-trip fares on flights from its U.S. gateway cities to Switzerland and other countries in Europe. Yours for the asking, it is available on flights all year round and every day of the week.

The second perk from this airline is a 10 percent discount for you and a companion, up to $100 per person, when you book a Swissair air/land package.

For information: Call your travel agent or 800-221-4750. For the land program, call Swisspak, 800-688-7947.

TAP AIR PORTUGAL

The discount you're qualified for from this airline if you are at least 62 is 10 percent off almost any fare on flights between the United States and Portugal, Madeira, and the Azores. The discount applies to a younger flying partner as well. Be prepared to present your passport or driver's license as proof of age. You may fly any time.

For information: Call your travel agent or 800-221-7370.

Chapter Eight

Beating the Costs
of Car Rentals

Never rent a car without getting a discount or a special promotional rate. Almost all car-rental agencies in the United States and Canada give them to all manner of customers, including those who belong to over-50 organizations (see Chapter 19) and airline senior clubs (see Chapter 7). The discount that's coming to you as a member can save you a lot of money. Refer to the membership material sent by the group to which you belong for specific information about your discount privileges.

But, first, keep in mind:

▶ Car-rental agents may not always volunteer information about senior discounts or special sales, so always ask for it.

▶ Don't settle for a senior discount or senior rate too hastily without investigating the possibility of an even better deal. Discuss your travel plans with a travel agent or car-rental agent and do some investigative work to find the *lowest available rate or package* at that moment. Even if you are entitled to a senior discount, special promotions or weekend rates are often better.

▶ When you reserve a car, always ask for a confirmation

number. When you pick up your car, always verify the discount and ask if a better rate has become available since you booked.

▶ When you call to ask about rates or reservations, always be armed with your organization's ID number and your own membership card for reference.

▶ The savings may not be available at all locations, so you need to check them out every time you make a reservation.

ADVANTAGE RENT-A-CAR

These car-rental agencies concentrated in the Southwest give a 10 percent discount to members of AARP.
For information: Call 800-777-5500.

ALAMO RENT A CAR

The Experienced Driver Discount—5 to 10 percent off the lowest available retail rate—is offered at all locations to members of AARP, Delta's Young at Heart program, United Silver Wings Plus club, Hilton Senior HHonors Club, Days Inns September Days Club, *and* anyone else who's over 50. A 24-hour advance reservation is required. Alamo offers additional senior specials every September, so if you are planning to travel at that time, check them out.
For information: Call your travel agent or 800-327-9633.

AVIS CAR RENTAL

Special rates amounting to 5 to 10 percent, sometimes more, off regular rates are given to members of AARP and CARP.

For information: Call your travel agent or 800-331-1800.

BUDGET RENT-A-CAR

Budget gives you a 5 to 10 percent discount at its U.S. locations if you belong to AARP or one of several other senior organizations. In Canada, CARP and AARP members pay a special rate that is always lower than the regular rate. As everywhere, ask whether there is a promotional rate that's better at that moment.

For information: Call your travel agent or 800-527-0700.

DOLLAR RENT A CAR

Discounts, which vary according to location but never fall below 5 percent, are offered to seniors, certainly at 65 and usually much earlier, depending on location.

For information: Call your travel agent or 800-800-4000.

ENTERPRISE CAR RENTALS

AARP members are entitled to 10 percent off the regular rental rates for compact cars or larger at Enterprise.

For information: Call your travel agent or 800-325-8007.

HERTZ CAR RENTAL

If you are a member of AARP, Y.E.S., the National Association of Retired Federal Employees, or the Retired Officers Association, you are entitled to savings, usually from 5 to 10 percent, on Hertz rental cars. In addition, Hertz gives discounts to members of United Silver Wings Plus.

For information: Call your travel agent or 800-654-3131.

NATIONAL CAR RENTAL

With this rent-a-car agency, you get a minimum 10 percent discount on all rentals if you are a member of AARP or CARP.

For information: Call your travel agent or 800-227-7368.

THRIFTY CAR RENTAL

Thrifty guarantees a 10 percent discount on the lowest rate you can get at any of its 600 locations in the U.S. and Canada if you are over 55. This is applied on top of almost any other discount for which you may qualify.

For information: Call your travel agent or 800-367-2277.

VALUE RENT-A-CAR

Merely show your AARP card and you will get a 5 percent discount at Value on compact or larger cars except during some blackout periods.

For information: Call 800-468-2583.

Chapter Nine

Saving a Bundle on Trains, Buses, and Boats in North America

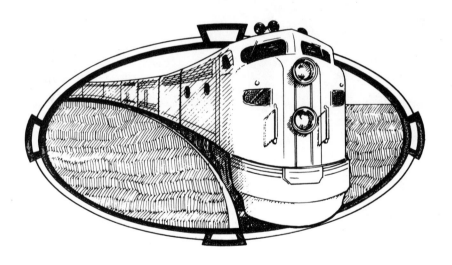

Getting around town, especially in a city where driving is not a practical option, probably means depending on public transportation to get you from hither to yon. Remember that, once you reach a particular birthday—in most cases, your 60th or 65th— you can take advantage of some good senior markdowns on trains, buses, and subways (unfortunately, taxis have yet to join the movement). All you need is a Medicare card, a Senior ID card, or your driver's license to play this game, which usually reduces fares by half. Although you may find it uncomfortable at first to pull out that card and flash it at the bus driver or ticket agent, it soon becomes easy; in addition, you will realize some nice savings.

And don't fail to take advantage of the bargains available to seniors on long-distance rail, bus, and boat travel as well.

RIDING THE RAILS

Probably every commuter railroad in the United States and Canada gives older riders a break, although you may have to do your traveling during off-peak periods when the trains are not filled with go-getters rushing to and from their offices. Ask for your discount when you purchase your ticket.

As for serious long-distance travel, many mature travelers are addicted to the railroads, finding riding the rails a leisurely, relaxed, romantic, comfortable, economical, and satisfying way to make miles while enjoying the scenery.

So many passes and discounts on railroads are available to travelers heading for other parts of the country that sorting them out becomes confusing. But, once you do, they will help stretch your dollars while covering a lot of ground.

See the country-by-country section in Chapter 4 for the best deals on trains in foreign countries for travelers of a certain age.

AMTRAK

To accommodate senior travelers, Amtrak offers a 15 percent discount on the lowest available coach fare, including All-Aboard America Passes, every day of the week (with a few holiday blackouts) to anyone 62 or older. The discount isn't available on the Auto Train, Metroliner Service, or some Canadian routes, but you may upgrade to first-class Club Service or sleeping accommodations using the senior coach fare as your base.

The lowest round-trip coach fares often sell out quickly, so always book train space well in advance. Not all fares are available on every train and some have restrictions.

Also, call 800-321-8684 for information about new fare reductions for over-62s on Amtrak's Air/Rail Travel Plans.

For information: Call Amtrak at 800-USA-RAIL (800-872-7245).

ALASKA RAILROAD

Passengers over 65 are entitled to a 25 percent reduction in fares during the winter months—late September through mid-May.

For information: Call Alaska Railroad at 800-544-0552.

VIA RAIL CANADA

The government-owned Canadian passenger railroad offers you, at age 60, 10 percent off the regular coach fare every day of the year with no restrictions. Add this 10 percent to the 40 percent reduction on off-peak travel, available to all ages and applicable any day of the week except Friday and Sunday, and you end up with tickets that are half price. Tickets at the off-peak rate must be purchased at least five or seven days in advance. However, the number of seats sold at this rate is limited, so plan ahead and buy your tickets as early as possible.

When you reach the age of 60, you are also eligible to buy a Canrailpass at discounted prices. The pass allows you to travel for any 12 days during a 30-day period anywhere on Via Rail's transcontinental system. You may board and deboard the train as many times as you wish, stopping wherever you like along the way.

For information: Via Rail Canada, PO Box 8116, Station A, Montreal, Quebec H3C 3N3. For reservations or a Canrailpass, call your travel agent or call 800-561-3949 (in Canada, consult your directory for the toll-free number).

GO BY BUS

Never, never board a bus without showing the driver your Senior ID card, because even the smallest bus lines in the tiniest communities in this country and abroad give senior discounts, usually half fare. In Europe, your senior rail pass is often valid on major motorcoach lines as well, so always be sure to ask.

GREYHOUND BUS LINES

If you decide to let Greyhound do the driving, you are entitled to a 15 percent reduction on any walk-up fares once you have passed your 55th birthday. Be prepared to show a photo ID with proof of age. But always keep in mind that Greyhound offers occasional specials, promotional fares that are even lower than you'll get with your senior discount, so be sure to ask for the *lowest available fare* at the time you want to travel. Your senior discount, by the way, may not be applied to promotional fares.

For information: Call your local Greyhound reservations office or 800-231-2222.

GREYHOUND LINES OF CANADA

In Canada, Greyhound will give you 10 percent off the regular adult fare any day of the week, all year around, if you are a traveler over the age of 60 with a valid ID. You are also eligible for discounts on special fare packages such as the Canada Travel Pass, which allows for unlimited travel and unlimited stops on Greyhound routes.

For information: Call Greyhound Lines of Canada, 800-661-8747 (in Canada only) or 403-265-9111.

GRAY LINE TOURS

Gray Line is an association of many small independent motorcoach lines throughout the country, all of which offer sight-seeing and package tours. Most, but not all, of them give a 15 percent discount on half- and full-day sight-seeing tours to members of AARP at age 50 and sometimes other seniors as well. Find out if you qualify before buying your ticket. You must buy your ticket at a Greyhound terminal or on board the bus from company personnel.

For information: Call the Gray Line Tours office in your area.

ONTARIO NORTHLAND

An excursion railroad that takes you on wilderness tours of Canada's north country through areas accessible only by rail or plane, Ontario Northland offers travelers 65 or older a 25 percent fare reduction any day of the year. Although it does not apply to package tours, it may be used for other travel on the line, including the Polar Bear Express, an excursion in Ontario's far north that operates from mid-June until Labor Day for which you'll get half-price fares.

For information: Ontario Northland, 65 Front St. West, Toronto, ON M5J 1E6; in Ontario and Quebec, 800-268-9281; elsewhere, 416-314-3750.

VOYAGEUR COLONIAL LTD.

This Canadian motorcoach line's Club 60 offers you a discount of 25 percent on the regular one-way bus fares throughout the provinces of Quebec and Ontario, without prior reservations, seven days a week. Simply present proof of your age when you buy your tickets. You will also get discounts of varying amounts on Voyageur's one-day bus or riverboat tours out of such major cities as Montreal, Ottawa, and Toronto.

A deal that may profit you even more than your senior discount, however, if you plan extensive travel in these provinces, is the TourPass that is available to all ages and may be used for 14 consecutive days from May 1 through October 26. Check it out.

For information: Voyageur Colonial Ltd., 505 De Maisonneuve Blvd. East, 3rd floor, Montreal, Quebec H2L 1Y4; 514-842-2281 in Montreal; 416-393-7911 in Toronto; 613-238-5900 in Ottawa.

GO BY BOAT

ALASKA MARINE HIGHWAY

Traveling on the Alaska Marine Highway during fall and winter is a bargain for foot passengers 65 and older. Between October and April, you sail for half the regular adult fare within Alaskan waters. This means you must leave from an Alaskan port and land at another. The discount does not apply to vehicle or cabin space.

For information: Call 800-642-0066.

TOURING BY BOAT, RAIL, BUS

THE ALASKAPASS

With an AlaskaPass, you may travel on many kinds of surface transportation in Alaska and the Yukon Territory for a specified number of days, using gateways in

British Columbia and the state of Washington. One set discounted price allows unlimited travel on participating ferries, buses, and trains. These include the Alaska Marine Highway ferries, the Alaskan Express Motorcoaches, the Alaska Railroad, Alaska Direct Bus Line, B.C. Rail, B.C. Ferries, Island Coach Lines, Greyhound Lines of Canada, and Norline Coaches (Yukon). You plan your own itinerary, make your own reservations, and pay for your transportation with the pass, using, if you like, suggested itineraries.

The off-season—October 1 through March 31—is when seniors get a good deal on the cost of the pass. Then, an AlaskaPass Travelpass costs 65-plus travelers $100 less than it costs other adults.

For information: Call your travel agent or AlaskaPass 800-248-7598.

Chapter Ten

Hotels and Motels: Get Your Over-50 Markdowns

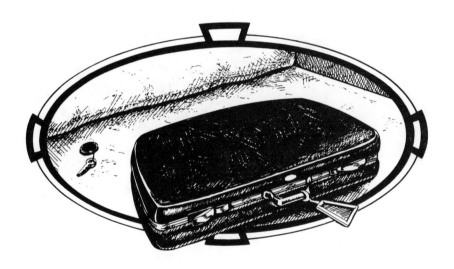

Across the United States and Canada and throughout the rest of the world, major chains of hotels and motels (and individual establishments as well) are chasing the mature market—that's you. As a candidate for an increasing barrage of bargains in lodgings, you may not have to sell the family jewels to afford your next trip.

You don't even have to wait until you're eligible for Social Security to get senior discounts at most hotels. Many large chains and most independent establishments offer them to travelers aged 50 or 55, usually requiring only proof of age or a membership card in a qualifying organization such as AARP. When you join a senior organization, you receive a list of the lodging chains that offer special rates to reward you for having lived so long and traveled so much. Other hotel chains give good discounts, sometimes as much as 50 percent off, to members of their own senior clubs that cost little or nothing to join and usually allow you to sign up at the front desk when you arrive at the hotel.

What all this means is that you should *never* make a hotel/motel reservation without making sure you are getting your senior privileges or an even better deal.

But, first, keep in mind:

If you want to take advantage of the discounts coming to you, be sure to do some advance research and planning with your travel agent or on your own.

▶ In this rapidly changing world, rates and policies can be altered in a flash, so an update is always advisable.

▶ Information about discounts is seldom volunteered. In most cases, you must arrange for discounts when you make your reservations and remind the desk clerk of them again when you check in. Do not wait until you're settling your bill because then it may be too late.

▶ Usually, over-50 discounts are subject to "space availability." That means it may be pretty hard to get them when you want to travel. So always book early, demanding your discount privileges, and try to be flexible on your dates in order to take advantage of them. Your best bets for space are usually weekends in large cities, weekdays at resorts, and non-holiday seasons.

▶ It's quite possible that a special promotional rate, especially in off-peak seasons or on weekends, may save you more money than your senior discount. Many hotels, especially in big cities and warm climates, cut their prices drastically in the summer, for example. Others that cater mostly to business people during the week try to encourage weekend traffic by offering bargain rates if you stay over a Saturday night. Resorts are often eager to fill their rooms on weekdays. So always investigate all the possibilities before you get too enthusiastic about using your hard-earned senior discount, and remember to ask for the *lowest available rate*.

▶ There are several chains of no-frills budget motels that don't offer discounts or too much in the way of amenities but do charge very low room rates and tend to be located along the most-traveled routes.

▶ In some cases, not every hotel or inn in a chain will offer the discount. Those that do are called "participating" hotels/motels. Make sure the one you are planning to visit is participating in the senior plan.

▶ In addition to the chains, many independent hotels and inns are eager for your business and offer special reduced rates. Always *ask* before making a reservation. Your travel agent should be able to help you with this.

▶ Some hotel restaurants will give you a discount too, usually whether or not you are a registered guest.

▶ By the way, your discount will not be given on top of other special discounts. One discount is all you get.

AMERICAN EXPRESS SENIOR MEMBERSHIP
The first senior-targeted credit card, American Express Senior Membership is a new "status of membership" for which all current cardmembers are eligible, and those 62 and over get a reduced annual fee of $35 ($55 for a Gold Card). The senior membership card gives you all of the usual benefits and services plus a quarterly newsletter, special savings on travel, shopping and dining, a 24-hour hotline for medical and legal referrals or for sending urgent messages back home, a 24-hour hotline to licensed pharmacists for questions about medications, and a reduction in the annual membership fee for SeniorNet.
For information: Call 800-323-8300.

ASTON HOTELS AND RESORTS

Aston's Sun Club gives travelers 55 and older—and their traveling companions—up to 25 percent off room rates at its 40 hotels and condominium resorts on Hawaii's major islands, plus a $10 credit per day (up to $50) toward the cost of a car rental. Ask for the special rates when you make your reservations and pick up a coupon book of discounts when you check in. Sun Club rooms are limited, so reserve early.
For information: Call 800-922-7866.

BEST INNS

At these inexpensive inns mainly in the Midwest and South, those over 50 are entitled to $5 off the room rate Monday through Saturday and $10 off on Sunday night if they belong to the free Senior First Club. Ask for an application at an inn or by calling the toll-free number.
For information: Call 800-237-8466.

BEST WESTERN INTERNATIONAL

Just show your AARP membership card at any participating Best Western anywhere in the world and you will get an automatic 10 percent discount off regular room rates and a room upgrade if it is available at check-in. To get a 15 percent discount, you must enroll at no cost in Best Western Seniority, a second program for AARP members, and make advance reservations through a toll-free number. With this plan, for every dollar you spend on room cost you will also earn points that are redeemable for travel awards and other benefits.

For information: Call 800-603-2277. To join Best Western Seniority, call 800-456-9719.

BUDGETEL INNS
At these inexpensive motels located mainly in the South and Midwest, you will get a 10 percent discount just for being over 55. You will get it at 50 if you are a member of AARP.
For information: Call 800-428-3438.

CANADIAN PACIFIC HOTELS & RESORTS
These first-class hotels and resorts scattered about Canada give a 30 percent discount on regular room rates, subject to availability, to card-carrying members of AARP and CARP.

Also, be sure to check out the special off-peak packages designed for older travelers at many Canadian Pacific hotels. For example: the Seniors Spring Fling, the Seniors Fall Getaway, the Sixty-Something room rate, and the Second Honeymoon.
For information: Call 800-441-1414.

CANADIAN ROCKY MOUNTAIN RESORTS
These three unique resorts—Deer Lodge in Lake Louise, Buffalo Mountain Lodge in Banff, and Emerald Lake Lodge in Yoho National Park—in the spectacular Canadian Rocky Mountains are loaded with charm, interesting decor, and scenery. In addition, they give discounts to seniors 65 and up: 10 percent in the high sea-

son, 25 percent in the regular season, and 50 percent in the low season.
For information: Call 800-661-1595.

CASTLE RESORTS & HOTELS
Castle's deluxe hotels and resort condominiums give visitors over the age of 55 a 30 percent discount on the regular room rates. They also offer special room-and-car packages.
For information: Call 800-367-5004.

CLARION CARRIAGE HOUSE INNS
See Comfort Inns.

CLARION HOTELS AND RESORTS
See Comfort Inns.

COLONY HOTELS AND RESORTS
Mainland hotels, a dozen Hawaiian properties on five islands, and hotels in Israel, Thailand, and Mexico give a 25 percent discount every day of the year to AARP members and 20 percent to others who are over 60. Advance reservations are a must.
For information: Call 800-777-1700.

COMFORT INNS
All 1,500 Comfort Inns take catering to older travelers very seriously, offering everyone over the age of 50 their Senior Saver rate. This means you get 30 percent off the

regular room rate when you make an advance reservation through your travel agent or by calling their toll-free number. Without advance reservations, you will get a 10 percent discount if a room is available. It pays to plan ahead.

Comfort Inns are part of Choice Hotels, an international group of more than 3,200 inns in 34 countries that also includes Clarion Hotels and Resorts, Clarion Carriage House Inns, Quality Inns, Sleep Inns, Friendship Inns, Econo Lodges, and Rodeway Inns. All of these hotels and inns give you the same Senior Saver rates.
For information: Call your travel agent or 800-221-2222.

CONRAD HOTELS

The international subsidiary of Hilton USA, Conrad Hotels in Europe, Australia, Mexico, Hong Kong, and the Caribbean participate in Hilton's Senior HHonors Program for over-60s. Members of the club are entitled to 25 to 50 percent off room rates. For more, see Hilton Hotels.

COURTYARD BY MARRIOTT

Here AARP members are in luck—they get up to 10 percent off the regular room rates as well as 15 percent off lunch and dinner (food and nonalcoholic beverages) at the hotel restaurants whether or not they are hotel guests. Nonmembers must be 62 to get the same 15 percent discount on lodging. Advance reservations are recommended.
For information: Call 800-321-2211.

CROSS COUNTRY INNS
Check in at one of these inns in Ohio, Kentucky, or Michigan and you will get 25 percent taken off the regular room rates if you belong to AARP, have a Golden Buckeye card, or are over 60.
For information: Call 800-621-1429.

CROWN STERLING SUITES
A group of all-suite hotels in the U.S., Crown Sterling Suites has introduced its Senior Savings Time, with special reduced rates for travelers over 60. You'll get $10 off the regular weekend rates every day of the week. What's more, you'll get a full breakfast every morning and complimentary drinks every evening.
For information: Call 800-433-4600.

DAYS INNS
One of the largest lodging chains in this country and abroad, Days Inns invites you at age 50 to join its September Days Club, entitling you to 15 percent to 50 percent off rooms at about 1,600 participating hotels, motels, suites, and lodges. You also get 10 percent off your meals at participating Days Inns restaurants and your purchases at its gift shops, discounts on rental cars, discounts on prescription and over-the-counter drugs, discounts on entertainment attractions and theme parks, trips at group rates, last-minute travel bargains, a travel magazine, and many more perks. The club costs $12 a year for you and your spouse. Members of the Canadian Snowbird Association get similar benefits. Most inns also give AARP members and everybody over

65 a 10 percent discount on rooms any day of the year.
For information: Call 800-325-2525.

DOUBLETREE HOTELS

Almost all Doubletree Hotels and Doubletree Club Hotels give members of AARP and anyone else over the age of 60 a good deal: 30 percent off the lowest available corporate rate on weekdays and 10 percent off the lowest available weekend rate. You'll also get 10 percent off food and nonalcoholic beverages in Doubletree restaurants and from room service if you are hotel guests.
For information: Call 800-528-0444.

DOWNTOWNER MOTOR INNS

See Red Carpet Inns.

DRURY INNS

These economy motels offer a 10 percent discount on the regular room rates at all of their 60 locations to anyone 50 or over. Just ask and have your proof of age handy.
For information: Call 800-325-8300.

ECONO LODGES

See Comfort Inns.

ECONOMY INNS OF AMERICA

This economy lodging chain, with motels located near major highways in California, Florida, South Carolina, and Georgia, gives 10 percent off the room rates to AARP members and anyone over 55. Just ask for it.
For information: Call 800-826-0778.

EMBASSY SUITES

Two-room suites with full breakfast and complimentary cocktails, all Embassy Suites hotels take at least 10 percent off the room rates—and sometimes more, depending on the location—for travelers with AARP cards.
For information: Call 800-362-2779.

FAIRFIELD INNS BY MARRIOTT

At Marriott's economy lodging chain, you will get 10 percent deducted from your bill if you belong to AARP.
For information: Call 800-228-2800.

FRIENDSHIP INNS

See Comfort Inns.

GUEST QUARTERS

A small chain with about 30 locations and suites with one or two bedrooms, Guest Quarters takes off 10 to 30 percent or more at most of its hotels for people over 65 or members of AARP or other senior groups.
For information: Call 800-424-2900.

HAMPTON INNS

The LifeStyle 50 program charges you the single rate for any room type you choose—with no additional cost for up to three others sharing your room—at any of the 425 Hampton Inns around the country. Just show proof that you are over 50 when you check in. You'll each get a complimentary continental breakfast.
For information: Call 800-426-7866.

HARLEY HOTELS
Look for a 10 percent discount at all of these hotels in the Northeast—except in New York City—simply by flashing your AARP or other senior organization card. On weekends, however, the weekend rate may be a better bet.

For information: Call 800-321-2323.

HAWAIIAN HOTELS AND RESORTS
At 55, you'll get a 30 percent discount off the regular rates plus a free room upgrade to the best available room at any of these hotels located on several islands in Hawaii and in California. You'll also receive a Value Card, good for food and beverage discounts and free or discounted activities.

For information: Call 800-222-5642.

HAWAIIAN PACIFIC RESORTS
This group's 12 hotels in Hawaii give varying discounts to travelers over 55, but most offer at least 40 percent off the regular rates. They also have room-and-car specials for older travelers at all of the properties, again varying by location, but definitely worth investigating if you want wheels.

For information: Call 800-367-5004.

HILTON HOTELS
Anybody who is at least 60 may enroll in Hilton's Senior HHonors travel program for an annual fee of $50 or a lifetime fee of $275 to get up to 50 percent off in 230

Hiltons in the U.S. and seven Conrad Hotels abroad. The membership includes you and your spouse. You may reserve an additional room at the same rate for family and friends who are traveling with you. And you will get 20 percent taken off the bill on dinner for two at participating hotel restaurants whether or not you are currently staying at the hotel.

For those who don't join the Senior HHonors travel program but do belong to AARP, most Hiltons honor a special discount that amounts to 10 or 15 percent.

For information: Call 800-445-8667. To enroll in the club, call 800-432-3600, extension 902.

HILTON INTERNATIONAL

The Senior Passport Program offered by Hilton International, with more than 160 hotels in 50 countries, gives special reduced nightly rates of $79, $109, $129, or $149 (depending on the location) to travelers over the age of 60. A maximum of two rooms can be booked under one senior's name for the same stay. A full American breakfast option is available for $8 a day.

To take advantage of the program, you must make advance reservations and show proof of your age when you check in.

For information: Call 800-HILTONS.

HOLIDAY INN

Holiday Inn Alumni, a new travel club for mature travelers, is a good bet if you're over 60 and spend much time on the road because members receive a minimum discount of 20 percent—and sometimes more—off the regular room rates at participating hotels. A continental breakfast comes with the room.

Not only that, but you'll have 10 percent deducted from all food purchases at breakfast, lunch, and dinner at any of the hotel restaurants, whether you are staying at the inn or just dropping by for a meal. On your birthday, you get a complimentary dinner, also whether you're currently a guest or not. During the Thanksgiving and Christmas holidays, the club rates and benefits are extended to members of your family too.

To join Holiday Inn Alumni, call the toll-free number below or sign up at a participating hotel. The first year is complimentary; after that, the membership costs $10 per year, a fee that is waived if you stay a minimum of five nights a year at any Holiday Inn. You are automatically enrolled if you were a member of the chain's former Preferred Traveler program or belong to certain senior organizations.

All is not lost if you don't join the club because with an AARP card, you are entitled to a discount of 10 percent off the regular room rates.

For information: Call 800-HOLIDAY for reservations. To enroll in the club, call 800-653-9473.

HOMEWOOD SUITES
This small group of hotels features moderate-priced apartment-style suites that, in most of its locations, are available to members of AARP at a discount of 15 percent off the regular rates.

For information: Call 800-225-5466.

HOWARD JOHNSON AND HOJO INNS

Howard Johnson offers card-carrying members of AARP a 20 percent discount on regular room rates at its nearly 600 hotels, inns, and lodges and a 15 percent discount to over-50 members of other senior organizations such as CARP *and* everyone else over the age of 60. Advance reservations are not necessary. Just check in at a participating inn in the U.S., Mexico, or Canada and show your ID.

Another good deal is the Howard Johnson Travel Saver Plus Club, which gives you a guaranteed 15 percent off standard room rates and often even larger discounts up to 50 percent at participating properties with or without reservations. You also get 10 percent off the bill at Howard Johnson's Restaurants and participating restaurants at HJ locations. In addition, discounts on trips, domestic and international tours and cruises, attractions, airline tickets, and rental cars, a travel magazine, and other services go along with membership, which costs $20 a year for you and your spouse.

For information: Call 800-446-4656. To join or receive more information about the HJ Travel Saver Plus Club, call 800-547-7829.

HYATT HOTELS AND RESORTS

Hyatt Hotels and Resorts in the U.S., Canada, and the Caribbean offer a nice, simple discount formula to mature travelers: 25 percent off the regular room rates for guests 62 or over. Simply ask for it when you make your reservations. The senior rate is subject to availability so, especially for stays during peak travel periods, be sure to reserve early.

For information: Call 800-228-9000.

KIMCO HOTELS

All of Kimco's hotels in cities on the West Coast, most of them in San Francisco, have something good to offer mature travelers. The senior packages at these small, moderately priced "boutique" hotels (each one different) give you discounts ranging up to 40 percent on the regular room rate and often include breakfast and evening wine service. You must be a member of AARP or at least 55 in most cases to qualify as a senior.

For information: Call 800-546-2622. Ask for the sales department.

KNIGHTS INNS/KNIGHTS STOPS/ ARBORGATE INNS

This budget motel chain with about 200 locations mostly in the East gives a discount of 10 percent throughout the year to anyone over 55 and AARP members at 50.

For information: Call 800-722-7220.

LA QUINTA MOTOR INNS

With about 200 locations in the U.S. and Mexico, these motor inns are inexpensive and become even more so when you ask for your 10 percent discount. You'll get it if you are a member of AARP or a similar organization or if you are 65 and can prove it.

For information: Call 800-531-5900.

LK INNS

A budget chain in the Midwest, LK takes 10 percent off for AARP members and anybody else over 55.

For information: Call 800-282-5711.

MARC RESORTS

If you are 60, a 25 percent discount is yours, except during holiday weeks, at Marc Resorts' 13 locations in the Hawaiian Islands.

For information: Call 800-535-0085.

MARRIOTT HOTELS, RESORTS, AND SUITES

Marriott's program for over-50s is among the best deals around if you are a member of AARP or CARP and can plan ahead. With an AARP or CARP membership card and a 21-day nonrefundable advance booking, you will get at least 50 percent off the regular rate at almost 200 participating locations. You must pay in advance for the entire stay by check or credit card when you make your reservation.

For those who can't commit themselves three weeks ahead, there is an automatic 10 percent discount on regular room rates every day of the year for AARP or CARP card carriers.

Both discounts apply to additional rooms if they are available, so family members or friends traveling with you can share your good fortune.

There is also a 20 percent discount on meals (except on specials and alcoholic beverages) at most of the hotels and resorts for your party of up to eight people. This may be used as often as you like, and you are not required to be an overnight guest to get this restaurant discount, but you must present your AARP or CARP card. Always ask first if the hotel or resort is participating in the discount plan.

And more: you'll get a 10 percent discount on gift-shop purchases at any of Marriott's hotels and resorts, except for certain items such as tobacco and candy.

Two hitches: the room discounts may not be available at all times, especially during peak periods, and some Marriotts do not participate in the seniors program.
For information: Call 800-228-9290.

MASTER HOSTS INNS
See Red Carpet Inns.

MOTEL 6
You can take advantage of a 10 percent discount on the room rates at Motel 6s, economy motels that can be found in more than 750 locations throughout the U.S.
For information: Call 800-440-6000.

NENDELS MOTOR INNS
A chain of inns on the West Coast, Nendels takes 10 percent off the regular room rates at most of its locations for members of all senior organizations and anyone over 55. The discount is also available at Value Inns by Nendels. Ask for it when you make your reservation or check in.
For information: Call 800-547-0106.

OMNI HOTELS
Omni Hotels are another winner in this series. The participating hotels in this group—about 45 of them in the United States and Mexico—offer AARP members a whopping 50 percent discount on regular room rates, based on space availability. You'll also get a 15 percent discount on food and nonalcoholic beverages in some of

their restaurants any time of day if you are a registered hotel guest and before 7 P.M. for dinner if you are not. To receive the special room rate, reserve ahead and request the discount. At check-in you will be asked to show your AARP membership card. In the restaurants, present it before you place your order.
For information: Call 800-843-6664.

OUTRIGGER HOTELS HAWAII
With hotels and condominium apartments all over the islands, Outrigger's Fifty Plus program offers you at age 50 a 20 percent discount off the regular room rates on all rooms at all times. For members of AARP, the discount is even better—25 percent. The discounts are yours for the asking if rooms are available.
For information: Call 800-733-7777.

PASSPORT INNS
See Red Carpet Inns.

QUALITY INNS
See Comfort Inns.

RADISSON HOTELS INTERNATIONAL
Anyone age 50 or older gets a senior rate that provides a minimum of a 25 percent discount. The senior discount is available every day of the week for a standard room, single or double, and includes family members traveling with you. You and family members accompanying you will also get 15 percent off your food and beverage bills

at the hotel restaurants, whether or not you are a hotel guest, if you are a member of AARP or United Silver Wings Plus, so carry your membership cards with you.
For information: Call 800-333-3333.

RAMADA INNS, HOTELS, AND SUITES

Ramada's Best Years Club, open to anyone over the age of 60 or a member of AARP, is good for a 25 percent reduction on the regular room rates at participating properties in the U.S. and Canada. It also gives members a quarterly newsletter; discounts on airfares, cruises, attractions, and car rentals; and 15 points for each dollar spent. Accumulated to specified levels, these points are redeemable for travel and merchandise awards. Lifetime membership in the club costs $15. Join at the front desk of any Ramada that is participating in the plan or call the number below.

A second choice at most Ramada hotels is a 15 to 25 percent discount on room rates for members of any of a long list of senior organizations, including AARP and United Silver Wings Plus, and anyone else over 60. Be prepared to present proof of your age and/or a membership card when you check in.
For information: Call 800-228-2828. To enroll in the club, call 800-672-6232.

RAMADA INTERNATIONAL HOTELS
AND RESORTS

These midscale hotels and resorts, all of them outside the U.S. and Canada, offer you their senior rate: 25 percent off the regular room rates every day of the year

if you belong to AARP or are over the age of 60. Ask for it when you make your reservations. Of course, rooms at the special rate are limited so make your plans early.
For information: Call 800-228-9898.

RED CARPET INNS
Almost all of the 350 Red Carpet Inns, Master Hosts Inns, Passport Inns, Downtowner Motor Inns, and Scottish Inns in the United States and Canada give AARP members or anybody else who's 55 a 10 percent discount on room rates year-round, except perhaps during special local events when available rooms are scarce.
For information: Call 800-251-1962.

RED LION HOTELS AND INNS
To over-50s who present AARP cards, Red Lions and Thunderbirds—all in the western states—give their Prime Rate, which amounts to 20 percent off the regular room rates. Book ahead, because there are occasional blackout periods. In addition, some of their restaurants give you 10 percent off food chosen from the regular menu, except on holidays.
For information: Call 800-547-8010.

RED ROOF INNS
Red Roof Inns, a large economy lodging chain with over 200 locations in 30 states, offers a program called RediCard +60. For a $10 fee, plus $2 for a spouse, you

may join the program for life at age 60, entitling you to a 10 percent discount on room rates, plus three coupons worth $5 each that are valid at any Red Roof Inn, a road map in its own travel pouch, a quarterly newsletter, and other privileges. Join when you check in.
For information: Call 800-843-7663.

RENAISSANCE HOTELS AND RESORTS
When you make reservations at any of the upscale Renaissance Hotels or Resorts, located in many countries around the world, ask for the senior rate if you are a member of AARP or over 60. Valid every day of the year, subject to availability, the discount amounts to 25 percent off the regular room rates. Make advance reservations because, as always, rooms at this special rate are limited in number.
For information: Call 800-228-9898.

RESIDENCE INNS BY MARRIOTT
Participating inns in this chain of all-suite accommodations designed for extended stays offer a 15 percent discount or more on the rates to members of AARP and CARP and anybody else over the age of 60.
For information: Call 800-331-3131.

RODEWAY INNS
See Comfort Inns. And check out Rodeway's new "senior-friendly" rooms.

SANDMAN HOTELS AND INNS
All situated in western Canada, these 20 inns take about 25 percent off the regular room rate if you are 55 or over. Show proof of age at check-in or, better yet, write in advance for a Club 55 Card: 1755 W. Broadway, Ste. 310, Vancouver, BC V6J 4S5. It's free.
For information: Call 800-726-3626.

SAS INTERNATIONAL HOTELS
This group of 30 hotels in nine countries in Europe and the Middle East gives special rates on weekends—Friday, Saturday, and Sunday nights—to people over the age of 65 and their roommates. The discount corresponds to your age. If you are 65, you receive a 65 percent discount on the room rate, while someone 100 gets a room for free—all, of course, subject to the availability of rooms. When you are traveling with another person, the older guest's age determines the size of the discount. Breakfast is included.
For information: Call 800-221-2350.

SCOTTISH INNS
See Red Carpet Inns.

SHERATON HOTELS, INNS, AND RESORTS
At all of the hundreds of Sheratons around the world, you will get a good break if you are over 60 or a member of AARP or CARP: 25 percent taken off the regular cost of a room, subject, of course, to availability. As always, it's a good idea to make advance reservations and carry proper identification.
For information: Call 800-325-3535.

SHONEY'S INNS
These inexpensive motels, about 60 of them, are concentrated in the South. Here, if you join the Merit Club 50 at age 50 or older, you will get a single-room rate for up to four guests to a room. Traveling alone? You get discounts that vary from inn to inn. Always ask for them. Sign up for the free club at an inn or over the telephone when you make your reservations.
For information: Call 800-222-2222.

SLEEP INNS
See Comfort Inns.

SONESTA INTERNATIONAL HOTELS
This collection of hotels, some in exotic locations, gives members of AARP and CARP and anyone else who is 65 a 10 percent discount off the regular rates. You must make reservations in advance, of course. Also check out Sonesta's seasonal specials, which may prove to be even better deals.
For information: Call 800-468-3571.

STOUFFER RENAISSANCE HOTELS AND RESORTS
First-class establishments throughout the U.S. and Mexico, this group gives anyone who's a member of AARP or is over 60 years of age a senior discount of 25 percent on the regular room rates any day of the week all year round. It's as simple as that. Advance reservations are always a good idea because rooms at this rate are limited to availability.
For information: Call 800-468-3571.

SUMMERFIELD SUITES

If you are at least 62, Summerfield Suites will give you a one-bedroom suite for $69 (regular rate is $99) and a two-bedroom for another $20. The special rates are available any time, any day of the week, but you must make advance reservations. The suites include a full kitchen, free buffet breakfast and social hour, free parking, and an on-site 24-hour convenience store.
For information: Call 800-833-4353.

SUPER 8 MOTELS

Many of the over 1,200 no-frills economy motels in this chain give a 10 percent discount to members of over-50 clubs or people over a certain age, that age differing according to the location.
For information: Call 800-843-1991.

SUSSE CHALETS

At most of these motels and inns scattered throughout New England and Maryland, you will get a 10 percent discount at age 60 if you ask for it.
For information: Call 800-258-1980.

SWISSOTELS

You'll get a senior discount, varying by location, at these upscale hotels in New York, Atlanta, Boston, and Chicago. To qualify, you must be an AARP member or at least 60 years of age.
For information: 800-621-9200.

THRIFTLODGE
These economy motels operated by Travelodge take 10 percent off your room rate simply because you are over the age of 50.
For information: Call 800-525-9055.

THUNDERBIRD MOTOR INNS
See Red Lion Hotels and Inns.

TRAVELODGE
Travelodge—all 450 of them in the U.S., Canada, and Mexico—has a nice straightforward plan for older travelers: an unrestricted 15 percent discount good any time, any night, for anybody who's over the age of 50. No membership cards to show, no advance reservations, and no blackout periods, but the discount is, of course, subject to availability of rooms.

Travelodge also offers its free Classic Travel Club for over-50s that has additional perks for you, among them discounts on car rentals. For instant enrollment, pick up an application at the front desk or call the reservations number.

And if you spend a lot of time on the road, be sure to note Travelodge's Guest Rewards program.
For information: Call 800-578-7878.

VAGABOND INNS
This group of inns, all in the West, has its Club 55 that gives discounts of 10 to 20 percent off single room rates

to guests who are over the age of 55. Club membership costs nothing and gets you coupons to be used toward a stay at any Vagabond Inn, a quarterly newsletter, and discounts on trips and social events. Just call to sign up. AARP members get discounts of 5 to 10 percent.

For information: Call 800-522-1555 in the U.S. In Canada, call 800-468-2251.

VALUE INNS BY NENDELS
See Nendels Motor Inns.

WELCOME INNS
Welcome, a small group of inns in Ontario and Quebec, gives members of AARP or CARP a senior rate that amounts to about 20 percent off the regular room rate, depending on the location. Nonmembers over 60 get a 10 percent discount.

For information: Call 800-387-4381.

WESTIN HOTELS AND RESORTS
These luxury hotels often offer senior rates, but each has its own policy, so always ask about the possibilities when you make your reservations. Members of United Silver Wings Plus, however, definitely get discounts of up to 50 percent. And if you are signed up for the Just for You package offered to American Express Senior Members, you are entitled to 5 to 30 percent off the lowest promotional rate for a standard room, plus 10 percent off lunch and dinner at participating hotel restaurants.

For information: Call 800-441-1414.

WYNDHAM HOTELS AND RESORTS

Ready for another really good deal? Wyndham Hotels in the U.S. give AARP members and anyone else over the age of 62 up to a 50 percent reduction on room rates. At the group's resorts in Bermuda, Jamaica, St. Lucia, and St. Thomas, AARP members and others over 62 are offered reduced rates that vary by the resort and the season but usually amount to about 20 percent.

For information: Call 800-WYNDHAM (800-996-3426).

GOOD DEALS IN RESTAURANTS

Many restaurants offer discounts to people in their prime, but in most cases you'll have to seek them out yourself, by asking or watching the ads in your local newspaper. In addition, a few large hotel chains will give you a break on your food bills when you eat in their restaurants. For example:

At most **Hilton Hotels** restaurants in the U.S. and Canada, you're entitled to a 20 percent discount on dinners for two, hotel guests or not, if you are a member of Hilton's Senior HHonors travel club.

Holiday Inn restaurants give a discount of 10 percent off your check when you dine there whether or not you are a guest at the inn if you belong to the Holiday Inn Alumni, a travel club for over-60s. On your birthday, your dinner will be free.

Take 10 percent off your bill at **Howard Johnson's Restaurants** and participating restaurants at HJ locations if you belong to the Howard Johnson Travel Saver Plus Club.

The restaurants in the participating **Marriott Hotels and Resorts** will take 25 percent off your bill for a party of up to eight people if you belong to AARP or CARP, whether or not you are staying at the hotel.

Doubletree Hotels and **Doubletree Club Hotels** take 10 percent off the bill for food and nonalcoholic beverages, both in their restaurants and on room service orders, for members of AARP or others over 60 who are guests at the hotel.

At most **Omni Hotels** you'll get 15 percent taken off the check for food and nonalcoholic beverages in the hotel restaurants by flashing your AARP card. The discount is yours at any hour if you are staying at the hotel, before 7 P.M. for dinner if you are not.

If you are a card-carrying member of AARP or United Silver Wings Plus, you get a reduction of 15 percent on your food and beverage bills for yourself and family members who accompany you when you eat at any of the **Radisson Hotel** restaurants. Valid whether or not you are a hotel guest.

Some of the restaurants at **Red Lion Inns** and **Thunderbird Motor Inns** will reduce your food bill by 10 percent on regular-priced items if you belong to AARP. Be ready to produce your membership card.

Chapter Eleven

Alternative Lodgings for Thrifty Wanderers

I f you're willing to be innovative, imaginative, and occasionally fairly spartan, you can travel for a song or thereabouts. Here are some novel lodgings that can save you money and, at the same time, supply you with adventures worth talking about for years. They are not all designed specifically for people over 50, but each reports that a good portion of its clientele consists of free spirits of a certain age who are looking to beat the high cost of travel, meet people from other places, and have a real good time.

For more ways to cut travel costs and get smart in the bargain, check out the residential/educational programs in Chapter 16.

AFFORDABLE TRAVEL CLUB

Join this bed-and-breakfast club for mature travelers and you'll pay a pittance for accommodations, meet interesting people, and see new places. You may join as a host member, putting up other travelers in your spare bedroom a couple of times a year and providing breakfast and a little of your time to acquaint your guests with your area. Visitors pay $15 for a single or $20 for a double per night for their stay. In return, you get to stay in other people's homes for the same token fee when you travel. Or you may prefer to be a nonhost member, using the guest privileges only and paying $25 for a single or $30 for a double per night.

There are currently about 800 host members in 40 states and 16 countries offering accommodations ranging from simple bedrooms to suites and condos. The annual host membership fee per household is $50, while a nonhost membership costs $90 a year. It entitles you to a directory that lists and describes the host homes and a quarterly newsletter. The club also sponsors a few group tours and home-stay programs every year.
For information: Affordable Travel Club, 6556 Snug Harbor Ln., Gig Harbor, WA 98335; 206-858-2172.

COLLEGE CAMPUSES
More than 700 colleges and universities in the United States, Canada, and Europe open their dormitories to travelers every summer. So do universities in Australia and New Zealand from mid-November until the middle of February, when their students are on summer break. They offer spartan but adequate student rooms at bargain prices—$15 to $30 a night—plus, in most cases, use of all campus facilities from swimming pool to cafeteria. Some include breakfast or, for not much more, three meals a day. Check with the colleges in the area you want to visit or get a copy of *U.S. and Worldwide Travel Accommodations Guide*, a compilation of campuses that offer guest lodgings. The rooms or apartments—and occasionally bedroom suites—are usually available by the day, the week, or the month.
For information and the directory: Campus Travel Service, PO Box 5486, Fullerton, CA 92635; 800-525-6333 or 714-525-6625.

DEL WEBB'S SUN CITIES

The three Sun Cities, operated by the Del Webb Corporation, offer affordable vacation getaway programs to show you the lifestyle of these retirement communities. The only requirements are that one of each visiting twosome is at least 55 years old and that they accompany a salesperson on a tour of the property some time during their stay.

The weekly vacation packages at Sun City West, outside of Phoenix, currently range from $199 to $499 per week per couple, depending on the season. They include a wine-and-cheese party and the use of all the recreational facilities, with a complimentary round of golf for two.

Sun City Las Vegas, 12 miles from the Strip, features stays of three, four, or seven nights in its new villas, for a cost at this writing of $195, $260, and $455 respectively. You may play a free round of golf, tour the model homes, use all the facilities, and eat a complimentary lunch.

And at Sun City Palm Springs, costs range from $115 to $510, depending on the season, for a stay of three, four, or six nights. Again you get a round of golf for two, the use of the facilities, a free lunch, a golf demonstration, and a tour of the property.

For information: Call 800-385-0027, extension 27.

EVERGREEN CLUB

This is a bed-and-breakfast club for singles or couples over 50 who have guest rooms in their homes that they're willing to make available to fellow club members traveling through their areas. No matter how elegant or simple your home is, no matter how close or far from the beaten path, the visitors pay $10 per night for single accommodations and $15 for double. You may not get rich on this venture, but you will meet a lot of interesting people. And, in return, you may stay in other people's homes at the same prices when you're on the road. The Evergreen Club now includes inexpensive, comfortable accommodations in more than 700 homes in the United States and Canada, along with a handful abroad and down under.

You pay $50 (per couple) or $40 (single) yearly dues. You'll get a membership card, an annual directory, and quarterly newsletters. The directory gives names and addresses of members, occupations and interests, policies about pets and smoking, and listings of nearby special attractions. Members make their own reservations and arrangements with one another.

For information: Send a self-addressed, stamped envelope to the Evergreen Club, 404 N. Galena Ave., Dixon, IL 61021; 800-374-9392 or 815-288-9600.

NEW PALTZ SUMMER LIVING

Consider spending a couple of the hottest months in the mountains, about 75 miles north of New York City. Every summer, while the usual student occupants are on vacation, 204 furnished garden apartments are reserved for seniors in the village of New Paltz, near Mohonk Mountain and home of a branch of the State University of New York. The rents at this writing for the entire summer (from early June until late August) range from $1,200 to $3,400, depending on the size of the apartment. Living right in town next to the campus, you may audit college courses free and attend lectures and cultural events. There are two heated pools and a tennis court in the complex, as well as a clubhouse. Buses travel to New York every Wednesday for those who want to go to the theater, and there are frequent day trips to places of interest.

For information: New Paltz Summer Living, 19 E. Colonial Dr., New Paltz, NY 12561; 914-255-7205.

OAKWOOD RESORT APARTMENTS

Travelers over 55 may take advantage of a Senior Snowbird package that gives them apartments for at least a 10 percent discount on the going rates. Choose among locations in California, Texas, Virginia, Las Vegas, Chicago, Detroit, Philadelphia, Memphis, and Denver. You must rent for a minimum of 30 days from November 1 through the end of April. All of the apartments are furnished, and the rents include weekly maid service and utilities. Most locations also have swimming pools, tennis courts, party rooms, fitness centers, and social activities.

For information: Oakwood Resort Apartments, R&B Realty Group, 2222 Corinth Ave., Los Angeles, CA 90064; 800-888-0103.

RETREAT CENTER GUEST HOUSES

If you are seeking a refuge from the pressures of daily life and time for quiet reflection, a stay at a retreat center guest house may be your answer. Retreat centers are church-affiliated compounds where guests of any persuasion (or none at all) and of any age may find lodging and three meals a day for an average of $35 a

day. *U.S. and Worldwide Guide to Retreat Center Guest Houses* describes more than 700 such centers in the U.S., Canada, Europe, New Zealand, and Australia.
For information: CTS Publications, PO Box 8355, Newport Beach, CA 92660; 714-720-3729.

ROYAL COURT APARTMENTS

As an alternative to hotels, studio apartments at the Royal Court in central London are available year-round. At this writing, double studios rent for $117 to $132 per night in low season. But you'll get a discount of 10 percent if you are over 50 and mention this book when you make your reservations.
For information: Royal Court Apartments, British Network Ltd., 594 Valley Rd., Upper Montclair, NJ 07043; 800-274-8583 or 201-744-5215.

SENIOR VACATION HOTELS OF FLORIDA

These four hotels take a novel approach: they provide senior sunlovers with vacation packages that include private accommodations, breakfast and dinner daily, parties, trips to attractions, sightseeing, and more. Current rates start at $800 (single) and $700 (per person double) for a month from May through October; more the rest of the year. The hotels are located in Bradenton, Lakeland, and St. Petersburg, and, while you will certainly be accepted at age 50, you'll fit into the group more easily if you're a little older than that.
For information: Senior Vacation Hotels of Florida, 7401 Central Ave., St. Petersburg, FL 33710; 800-223-8123.

SENIORS ABROAD

Now more than 10 years old, Seniors Abroad is an international home-stay program exclusively for people over 50, offering opportunities to live in the homes of hosts in foreign countries and learn firsthand about their families and communities. All hospitality is voluntary on the part of the hosts and without cost to the guests. Programs in Japan, Australia, New Zealand, Denmark, Sweden, and Norway include a minimum of three home stays of six days each. The costs of the programs are reasonable and cover international travel and hotel stays for orientation. Americans may volunteer to host travelers from these countries when they visit the U.S.

For information: Seniors Abroad, 12533 Pacato Circle North, San Diego, CA 92128; 619-485-1696.

SERVAS

Servas is an "international cooperative system of hosts and travelers" established to help promote world peace, goodwill, and understanding among peoples. A nonprofit, nongovernmental, interracial, and interfaith organization open to all ages, it provides approved travelers with lists of hosts (and their special interests) all over the world, including the United States. To participate, you make your own arrangements to visit hosts, usually for two days at a time, in their homes. No money changes hands. The hospitable people who offer to share their space with you are eager to learn about you and your culture. You may do the same for other travelers in return, if you wish.

Travelers must pay a membership fee of $55 per year

and are asked for two letters of reference and an interview. Hosts are interviewed and asked for a voluntary donation of $25 or more per year.

For information: Send a #10 self-addressed, stamped envelope to US Servas, 11 John St., Room 407, New York, NY 10038; 212-267-0252.

SUN CITY CENTER

Between Tampa and Sarasota, Florida, Sun City Center wants you to discover what a large, self-contained retirement town is all about and offers an inexpensive vacation package so you can sample the life there. You may stay for a few days or a week or more. At this writing, a stay of four days/three nights with daily continental breakfast, tennis, swimming, and club facilities costs $89 per couple from April 1 through January 15 and $177 from January 16 through April 15. A round of golf costs extra, but this is the home of the Ben Sutton School of Golf and offers 126 holes. The only hitch: you must take a tour of the town accompanied by a salesperson.

For information: Sun City Center, PO Box 5698, Sun City Center, FL 33571-5698; 800-237-8200.

TRAVELCLUB BED & BREAKFAST

This bed-and-breakfast club, an affiliate of the Evergreen Club, is similar to its mother organization, but its approximately 350 members throughout the United States are over-50s who want to know where to find inexpensive B&B lodgings in other people's homes without having to play host to travelers in return. Current overnight rates are $18 single and $24 double, including breakfast. Yearly club membership costs $40 for a single person, $50 for a couple. You will receive a host directory, updates, and a newsletter and will make your own arrangements.

For information: Send a stamped self-addressed business-size envelope to TravelClub, 404 N. Galena Ave., Dixon, IL 61021; 800-374-9392 or 815-288-9600.

Chapter Twelve
Perks in Parks and Other Good News

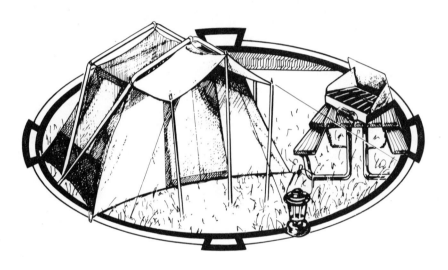

Here and there throughout the United States and Canada, enterprising states, provinces, and cities have thought up some enticing ideas designed to capture the imagination of the mature population. Often they are expressing their appreciation of our many contributions to society and simply want to do something nice for us. And sometimes they are trying to lure a few of our vacation dollars to their vicinity, having discovered that we're always out for a good time and know a good deal when we see one.

But, first, keep in mind:

▶ Before you set forth to visit a new area, it's a good idea to write ahead for free maps, calendars of events, booklets describing sites and scenes of interest, accommodation guides, and perhaps even a list of special discounts or other good things that are available to you as a person in your prime.

▶ Many states offer passes to their state parks and recreation facilities free or at reduced prices to people who are old enough to have learned how to treat them properly.

After the section on national parks, state park passes and other notable events are described for each state on the following pages. There may be other good deals that have escaped our attention, but those in this chapter are probably the cream of the crop.

ESCAPEES CLUB
Escapees is a club dedicated to providing a support network for RVers, full-time or part-time, most of whom are on the far side of 50. It publishes a monthly newsletter filled with useful information for travelers who carry their homes with them, organizes rallies in the U.S., Canada, and Mexico, and hosts five-day seminars on RV living. Other benefits include discounted co-op RV parks and campgrounds, emergency road service, and mail/message services. After a $10 fee to join, the annual membership fee is $40 a year.

The club has recently established its own CARE Center (Continuing Assistance for Retired Escapees), a separate RV campground where retired members can live independently in their own RVs while receiving medical and living assistance, housekeeping, and transportation services as needed.

For information: Escapees Inc., 100 Rainbow Drive, Livingston, TX 77351; 409-327-8873.

NATIONAL PARKS

GOLDEN AGE PASSPORT
Available for $10 to anyone over 62, this lifetime pass admits you free of charge to all of the federal government's parks, forests, refuges, monuments, and recreation areas that charge entrance fees. Anybody who

accompanies you in the same noncommercial vehicle also gets in free. If you turn up at the gate in a commercial vehicle such as a bus, the passport admits you and your spouse, your children, and your parents too, so remember to take them along.

You will also get a 50 percent discount on federal use fees charged for facilities and services such as camping, boat launching, parking, or cave tours.

The passport is not available by mail. You must pick one up in person at any National Park System area where entrance fees are charged or at any offices of the National Park Service, the U.S. Forest Service, the Fish and Wildlife Service, or the Bureau of Land Management. You must have proof of age. A driver's license will do just fine.

(The free Golden Access Passport provides the same benefits for the disabled of any age. The Golden Eagle Passport, for those under 62, costs $25 per year.)

For information: National Park Service, PO Box 37127, Washington, DC 20013.

CANADIAN NATIONAL PARKS

All you have to do to get free entry for day visits is to show your driver's license and vehicle registration. The same is generally true for provincial parks, with half-price camping fees charged on the weekends.

OFFERINGS FROM THE STATES

For a free listing of all the state tourism offices and their toll-free numbers, send a self-addressed, stamped envelope to Discover America, Travel Industry Association of America, 1100 New York Ave. NW, Ste. 450, Washington, DC 20005-3934.

COLORADO

The Aspen Leaf Pass entitles Colorado residents 62 and over to free entrance to state parks any day and camping on weekdays. The pass costs $10 per year.

For information: Colorado Division of State Parks, 1313 Sherman St., Room 618, Denver CO 80203; 303-866-3437.

CONNECTICUT

Residents of Connecticut who are over 65 get a free lifetime Charter Oak Pass that gets them into state parks and forests plus Gillette Castle, Dinosaur Park, and Quinebaug Valley Hatchery for free. In fact, their whole carload may enter the parks without charge. To get your pass, write to the address below and send along a copy of your current Connecticut driver's license.

For information: Charter Oak Pass, State Parks Division, DEP, 79 Elm St., Hartford, CT 06106-5127; 203-566-2304.

INDIANA

The Golden Hoosier Passport admits Indiana residents over the age of 60 and fellow passengers in a private vehicle to all state parks and natural resources without charge. An application for the Passport, which costs $5 a year, is available at state parks or from the Indiana State Parks Department.

For information: Indiana State Parks Dept., 402 W. Washington St., Room W298, Indianapolis, IN 46204; 317-232-4124.

MAINE
Pick up your free Senior Citizen Pass and you will pay no day-use fees at Maine state parks and historic sites. The pass is available at any state park or by writing to the Bureau of Parks and Recreation and including a copy of a document that proves your age.
For information: Maine Bureau of Parks and Recreation, State House Station 22, Augusta, ME; 207-287-3821.

MISSOURI
Missouri residents over the age of 60 are entitled to a free Silver Citizen Discount Card that gives them discounts at restaurants, stores, services, pharmacies, and other businesses throughout the state.
For information: Missouri Dept. of Social Services, PO Box 1337, Jefferson City, MO 65102-1337; 800-235-5503.

NEW HAMPSHIRE
Seniors Week at Mt. Washington Valley, in the White Mountains of New Hampshire, takes place every September just after Labor Day. Here, in the villages of Eaton, Conway, North Conway, Bartlett, Glen, Madison, and Jackson, everyone over the age of 55 is entitled to discounted lodging prices (10 to 30 percent off), restau-

rant specials, retail discounts, and an array of events and activities. Among the activities at discount rates are golf and lunch at the area's golf resorts, luncheon aboard the local railroad's dining car, ballroom dancing, wagon rides, and horseback riding. Other attractions include scenic drives, outlet shopping, tennis, hiking, and mountaintop views.

For information: Mt. Washington Valley Visitors Bureau, PO Box 2300, North Conway, NH 03860; 800-367-3364 or 603-356-5701.

NEVADA

Mature travelers to Nevada's capital, Carson City, can write or phone to join a free Seniors Strike Silver Club, which offers a long list of discounts and other good deals at local motels, shops, casinos, restaurants, and service establishments.

For information: Carson City Convention & Visitors Bureau, 1900 S. Carson St., Carson City, NV 89701; 800-638-2321.

NEW MEXICO

For a list of senior discounts for attractions, stores, hotels, restaurants, and transportation in Albuquerque, call the toll-free number below.

For information: Albuquerque Convention & Visitors Bureau; 800-284-2282.

NEW YORK

Simply by presenting your current valid New York driver's license or a New York nondriver's identification card, you will be entitled to all of the privileges of the Golden Park Program for residents over the age of 62. The program offers, any weekday except holidays, free vehicle access to state parks and arboretums, free entrance to state historic sites, and reduced fees for state-operated swimming, golf, tennis, and boat rentals. Just show your driver's license or ID card to the guard of each facility as you enter.

For information: State Parks, Albany, NY 12238; 518-474-0456.

OHIO

Residents of Ohio who are 60 or over may apply for a Golden Buckeye Card, which entitles them to discounts, typically about 10 percent, on goods and services at participating businesses throughout the state. Applications are available at local sign-up sites.

For information and the sign-up site nearest your home: Golden Buckeye Card Section, Ohio Dept. of Aging, 50 W. Broad St., 8th floor, Columbus, OH 43266-0501; 800-422-1976.

PENNSYLVANIA

The City of Philadelphia publishes a booklet, *Philadelphia Seniors on the Go*, that lists discounts available year-round to mature people in that city, from transportation to hotels, museums, restaurants, and cultural events. Get yours, go places, and save money.

For information: Philadelphia Visitors Center, 16th and John F. Kennedy Blvd., Philadelphia, PA 19102; 800-537-7676.

The Pennsylvania Dutch country, which has become one of America's favorite tourist areas, will send you a 36-page map and visitor's guide plus a free list of places—restaurants, hotels, motels, attractions—that offer discounts to seniors.
For information: Pennsylvania Dutch Convention and Visitors Bureau, 501 Greenfield Rd., Lancaster, PA 17601; 800-PA-DUTCH (800-723-8824).

SOUTH CAROLINA

The Golden Age Card is an identification pass for senior residents of South Carolina. It allows any resident over 65 free use of many facilities in state parks plus half off on camping fees.
For information: South Carolina Department of Parks, Recreation, and Tourism, 1205 Pendleton St., Columbia, SC 29201; 803-734-0166.

TENNESSEE

Travelers over the age of 62, residents of the state or not, are given 25 percent off the regular fees for camping in Tennessee's state parks and 10 percent off the room rates at the Resort Park Inns.
For information: Department of Tourist Development, 320 6th Ave. North, PO Box 23170, Nashville, TN 37202; 615-741-2159.

UTAH

The Silver Card, issued by Park City, an old mining town known for its great ski mountains, is a summer program of discounts that gives you 10 percent or more off on merchandise, tickets, and meals. Pick up your card at a participating hotel or inn. Plan to attend a Summer Senior Orientation and the annual Senior Picnic in the Park.

For information: Park City Convention and Visitors Bureau, 1910 Prospector Ave., Park City, UT 84060; 800-453-1360 or 801-649-6100.

GOOD SAM CLUB

The **Good Sam Club** is an international organization of RVers, mentioned here because the vast majority of people in rolling homes is over 50. This club can be very handy and reassuring when you're cruising the country. Among its benefits are 10 percent discounts on fees at thousands of campgrounds and on propane gas, RV parts, and accessories. In addition, it offers a lost-key service, lost-pet service, trip routing, mail-forwarding service, telephone-message service, a magazine, caravan gatherings, and campground directories. Probably the most important benefit is the emergency road service available to members because it includes towing for any vehicle, no matter how large. That's hard to get. Also, there are Good Sam travel tours all over the world, many of them "caraventures." And not least, about 2,200 local chapters hold regular outings, meetings, and campouts. Membership costs $19 a year per family.

For information: The Good Sam Club, PO Box 6888, Englewood, CO 80155-6888; 800-234-3450.

VERMONT

Vermont's residents over 60 may purchase a Green Mountain Passport for $2 from their own town clerk. It is good for a lifetime and entitles them to free day-use

admission at any Vermont State Park and its programs. Other benefits include discounts on concerts, restaurant meals, prescriptions, and more.
For information: Vermont Dept. of Aging, 103 S. Main St., Waterbury, VT 05676; 802-241-2400.

VIRGINIA
In this state that abounds with historical sites, you'll find senior discounts almost everywhere you go. You'll get them, for example, at Colonial Williamsburg, Busch Gardens, Berkeley Plantation, Mount Vernon, Woodlawn Plantation, Gunston Hall Plantation, the Edgar Allan Poe Museum in Richmond, and the Virginia Air and Space Center.
For information: Virginia Division of Tourism, 1021 E. Cary St., Richmond, VA 23219; 800-786-4484.

WASHINGTON, D.C.
The Golden Washingtonian Club is a discount program in the nation's capital for people over 60. With proof of age, both residents and visitors may get discounts from about 1,000 merchants listed in the *Gold Mine Directory,* free at many hotels or at the Washington Visitor Information Center. More than 30 hotels offer 10 to 40 percent off regular rates, many restaurants take a percentage off meals, and many retail stores do the same for purchases.
For information: D.C. Committee to Promote Washington, 1212 New York Ave. NW, Washington, DC 20005; 202-724-4091.

WEST VIRGINIA

Everybody who turns 60 in West Virginia gets a Golden Mountaineer Discount Card, which entitles the bearer to discounts from more than 3,500 participating merchants and professionals in the state and a few outside of it. If you don't receive a card automatically, you may apply for one. Flash it wherever you go and save a few dollars.

For information: West Virginia Commission on Aging, 1900 Kanawha Blvd. East, Charleston, WV 25305; 304-558-3317.

Chapter Thirteen
Good Deals for Good Sports

Real sports never give up their sneakers. If you've been a physically active person all your life, you're certainly not going to become a couch potato now—especially since you've probably got more time and energy, and maybe funds, than you ever had before to enjoy athletic activities. Besides, you can now take advantage of some enticing special privileges and adventures offered exclusively to people over 49.

The choices outlined here are not for those whose interest in sports is limited to reclining in comfortable armchairs in front of television sets and watching football games, or settling down on hard benches in stadiums with cans of beer. They are for peppy people who do the running themselves.

Don't forget to check out the courses and trips included among Elderhostel's hundreds of low-cost residential academic programs. Here you will find classes in many outdoor activities, such as golf, canoeing, hiking, skiing, biking, rafting, yoga, dance, tennis, aerobics, and flyfishing.

SPORTING VACATIONS

NATIONAL SENIOR SPORTS ASSOCIATION (NSSA)

An organization whose purpose is to encourage sports participation among people over 50, NSSA sponsors recreational and competitive golf vacations and tournaments in this country and abroad. Its four-day golf holidays are scheduled once or twice a month, following the sun to courses all over the continental U.S. In addition, it also organizes golf trips, usually for a week and sometimes 10 days, to locations overseas. Recent adventures included Scotland, Ireland, Mexico, Canada, the Caribbean, and Hawaii. Cruises to Caribbean islands and Bermuda, where you stop to play a few rounds, are also offered every year or so.

Other NSSA activities include bowling and tennis trips. Membership—$25 for one year, $65 for three years—entitles you to participate in the sports events and trips and also gets you a monthly newsletter, discounts on sporting equipment, and names and addresses of members so you can put a match together when traveling on your own.

For information: NSSA, 167 Old Post Rd., Southport, CT 06490; 800-282-6772.

ALL ADVENTURE TRAVEL

Check out this broad-spectrum agency (see Chapter 3) that specializes in active vacations centered around biking, hiking, walking, paddling, snorkeling, diving, kayaking, and sailing and such. It represents over 100 tour operators (some of which are listed separately in this book) and offers hundreds of adventurous trips, some designed specifically for over-50s and others suitable for older travelers as well as travelers of other ages. **For information:** All Adventure Travel, 5589 Arapahoe, Ste. 208, Boulder, CO 80303; 800-537-4025.

AMERICAN WILDERNESS EXPERIENCE

Action vacations are the specialty of AWE (see Chapter 3), an agency that offers trips from a great many tour operators (some are mentioned separately in this book). You will get a choice of adventures ranging from horseback trips to sailing, canoeing, kayaking, hiking, trekking, dog sledding, scuba diving, biking, cross-country skiing, and other vigorous options.
For information: American Wilderness Experience, Inc., PO Box 1486, Boulder, CO 80306; 800-444-0099 or 303-444-2622.

MT. ROBSON ADVENTURE HOLIDAYS

Adventurous over-50s are the exclusive participants in this tour operator's special trips that take place high in the Canadian Rockies several times every summer. Among the outings are hiking/canoeing vacations and heli-camping trips, all of which require you to be in good condition, athletic, and game. See Chapter 3 for more details.
For information: Mt. Robson Adventure Holidays, Box 146, Valemount, BC V0E 2Z0; 604-566-4351.

ELDERCAMP AT CANYON RANCH

ElderCamp is a seven-day health and fitness program for over-60s at Canyon Ranch, upscale fitness resorts in Tucson and the Berkshires. The purpose is to show you how to make positive changes in your lifestyle. A combination of education and exercise, the program includes daily aerobics and stretching; morning walks; sports; sessions with physicians, nutritionists, and therapists; relaxation instruction; group sessions on relevant issues; medical evaluations; and three healthy meals a day. Canyon Ranch also offers other fitness sessions for all ages, with guests over 60 getting a 10 percent discount in the winter in the Berkshires and in the summer in Arizona. **For information:** Canyon Ranch, 8600 E. Rockcliff Rd., Tucson, AZ 85715, or 91 Kemble St., Lenox, MA 01240; 800-726-9900.

OUTDOOR VACATIONS FOR WOMEN OVER 40

Any reader of this book is certainly over 40 and therefore qualifies, if female, for the trips organized by this adventure company founded by Marion Stoddart, an avid outdoorswoman and conservationist who likes to hike, bike, camp, ski, raft, and canoe with contemporaries. Trips are from only a couple of days to two weeks or even 17 days. Some are planned as multigenerational trips for mothers, daughters, grandmothers, granddaughters, aunts, and nieces; one participant must be over 40 and the other over 21. Accommodations vary from charming country inns, rustic lodges, and chateaus to windjammer bunks or sleeping bags under the stars.

Current adventures include a windjammer cruise in the British Virgin Islands, hiking and barging in Holland, hiking and rafting in Colorado, walking in Ireland, boating in Turkey, and cross-country skiing in Yosemite National Park.

For information: Outdoor Vacations for Women Over 40, PO Box 200, Groton, MA 01450; 508-448-3331.

THE OVER THE HILL GANG

This international club for energetic people on the far side of 50 began as a ski club (three former Colorado ski instructors were looking for company on the slopes; see Chapter 14), but its members can now be found participating in all kinds of athletic endeavors. Its literature states that it is "an organization for active, fun-loving, adventurous, enthusiastic, young-thinking persons. The only catch is, you have to be 50 or over to join." Spouses may be younger, however. You don't have to be a super-jock to be a member, but you do have to like action.

Right now, the club has about 3,300 members in 50 states and 14 countries and 12 Gangs (chapters) coast to coast. When there's no Gang in your vicinity, you may become a member at large and join in any of the goings-on. These include ski trips, scuba diving, hiking, vacation trips, camping and fishing, ballooning, surfing, canoeing, and more. Each Gang decides on its own activities. Just plain travel is on the agenda too.

The annual fee ($37 per single, $60 per couple) for national membership plus chapter dues, if you have a chapter in your area, gives you a news magazine, chapter and national event information and schedules, discounts, and a chance to join the fun.

For information: Over the Hill Gang International, 3310 Cedar Heights Dr., Colorado Springs, CO 80904; 719-685-4656.

BONUSES FOR BIKERS

Biking is becoming one of America's most popular sports, and people who never dreamed they could go much farther than around the block are now pedaling up to 50 miles in a day. That includes over-the-hill bikers as well as youngsters of 16, 39, or 49. In fact, some tours and clubs in the U.S. and Canada are designed especially for over-50s.

COUNTRYROADS BIKE TOURS

Bike tours in the Canadian province of Ontario are the specialty of this company whose escorted cycle holidays include two-day midweek trips for bikers over 50. Among them are a tour of Prince Edward County, a trip around Niagara Falls and the nearby wineries, and a spin through the farmlands and markets of Ontario's Mennonite country. You'll spend the nights at small inns or hotels. The tours are all-inclusive, bicycle and all. Countryroads also hosts longer trips offered by Elderhostel Canada.

For information: Countryroads Bike Tours, PO Box 70657, 2938 Dundas St. West, Toronto, ON M6P 4E7; 416-761-1844.

THE CROSS CANADA CYCLE TOUR SOCIETY

A nonprofit society for retired people and others who want to remain active as recreational cyclists, this group sponsors cycling trips, mainly in British Columbia, for its members, most of whom are over the age of 60. Twice a week, local members gather for long day rides, and several times a year the club sponsors longer trips to places like Alaska, Utah, the Canadian Rockies, Arizona, Hawaii, and New Zealand. Says the society, "Our aim is to stay alive as long as possible." Now that's a worthy goal.

For information: Cross Canada Cycle Tour Society, 6943 Antrim Ave., Burnaby, BC U5J 4M5; 604-433-7710.

ELDERHOSTEL'S INTERNATIONAL BICYCLE TOURS

Elderhostel, famous for its educational travel programs on the campuses of colleges and universities, also offers international bicycle tours that combine biking 25 to 35 miles a day with lectures by guides who accompany each trip and guest lecturers from local universities. You bike as a group but at your own pace, with regular stops for tours, talks, site visits, snacking, and relaxing. Three-speed bikes are provided, as are breakfast and dinner. Accommodations are in clean, simple, double hotel rooms, most with private baths. A van travels with you to carry the luggage and bike equipment. It will also give you a ride if you decide you can't possibly make it up one more hill.

There are weekly departures hosted by IBT (see below) from April through September to England's East Anglia, Denmark, Austria, the chateaux country of France, and the tulip country in the Netherlands. The moderate cost covers airfare and just about everything else except lunches.

For information: Elderhostel, 75 Federal St., Boston, MA 02110; 617-426-7788.

INTERNATIONAL BICYCLE TOURS

The Fifty Plus Tour run by IBT is planned for people over 50 who are not into pedaling up mountains but love to cycle. The trip goes to Holland in May and takes you on a leisurely pedal along bicycle paths and quiet country roads on flat terrain through farmland and quaint villages. You'll cover only about 30 miles a day, so there is plenty of time for sightseeing, snacking, shopping, and relaxing. Although this is the only tour strictly limited to over-50s, many older bikers are found on IBT's other bike tours to Holland, Denmark, England, France, Bermuda, Austria, Cape Cod, and Florida. And, of course, many more sign on for Elderhostel's bike tours (in England, France, the Netherlands, Austria, and Denmark), all hosted by IBT.

For information: International Bicycle Tours, PO Box 754, Essex, CT 06426; 203-767-7005.

ONTARIO MASTERS CYCLING ASSOCIATION

This is a biking club with members from all over the Canadian province of Ontario, most of them over 40 and some of them into their high 70s. It is primarily a racing club and organizes 12 events a year within the province, including time trials of 40 and 80 kilometers as well as pursuit and road races of 60 kilometers.

But the club also organizes bike tours for ordinary nonracing persons of both sexes. And you don't even have to be a formal member to join them—just show up at the start and ride. Among its other enticements, there are social get-togethers, a monthly newsletter listing upcoming events, and tips on buying good bikes and finding good meals en route.

For information: Ontario Masters Cycling Association, John Bonfield, 5 Waterloo St., Brantford, ON N3T 3R5.

WANDERING WHEELS
A program with a Christian orientation, Wandering Wheels runs long-distance bike tours in this country and abroad, including its 40-day Breakaway Coast-to-Coast for people who are "middle age or older." Its literature says, "The program carries a strong Biblical emphasis." For information: Wandering Wheels, PO Box 207, Upland, IN 46989; 317-998-7490.

BICYCLE RACING
Now we're leaving recreational pedaling behind and getting into really serious stuff. So, unless you're a dedicated racer who's in terrific shape, feel free to skip this section.

UNITED STATES CYCLING FEDERATION
The United States Cycling Federation is a racing organization that conducts amateur bicycle races for members between the ages of 9 and 89. It's composed of almost 2,000 member clubs throughout the country that promote activities for beginners and run their own races for the more experienced.

Some races require a USCF license, but many are open to all who wish to participate at $5 per day (plus $5 for insurance). Everyone starts in the entry-level category, then is upgraded appropriately. Riders over the age of 30 are divided into five-year incremental classes and compete against peers. Women do not race against men but form their own age groups.

USCF members receive a monthly publication that lists the upcoming events. The clubs and local bike shops also can provide information about races.

For information: USCF, 1 Olympic Plaza, Colorado Springs, CO 80909; 719-578-4581.

TENNIS, ANYONE?

An estimated four million of the nation's tennis players are over 50, with the number increasing every year as more of us decide to forego rocking chairs for a few fast sets on the courts. You need only a court, a racquet, a can of balls, and an opponent to play tennis, but, if you'd like to be competitive or sociable, you may want to get into some senior tournaments.

UNITED STATES TENNIS ASSOCIATION

The USTA offers a wide variety of tournaments for players over the advanced age of 35, at both local and national levels. To participate, you must be a member ($25 per year). When you join, you will become an automatic member of a regional section, receive periodic schedules of USTA-sponsored tournaments and events in your area for which you can sign up, get a discount on tennis books and publications, and receive a monthly magazine and a free subscription to *Tennis* magazine.

In the schedule of tournaments, you'll find competitions listed for specific five-year age groups: for men from 35 to 85-plus and for women from 35 to 80-plus.

There are also self-rated tournaments that match you up with people of all ages who play at your level. If you feel you're good enough to compete, send for an application and sign up. There is usually a modest fee.
For information: USTA, 70 W. Red Oak Lane, White Plains, NY 10604-3602; 914-696-7000.

USTA LEAGUE TENNIS, SENIOR DIVISION
If you want to compete with other 50-plus tennis players in local, area, and sectional competitions that culminate in a national championship, join the Senior Division of the USTA League Tennis program. Your level of play will be rated in a specific skill category ranging from beginner to advanced, and you'll compete only with people on your own ability level. Sign up in your community or write to the USTA for details.
For information: USTA, 70 W. Red Oak Lane, White Plains, NY 10604-3602; 914-696-7000.

USTA SENIOR NATIONAL CHAMPIONSHIPS
These tournaments are for serious senior players who are USTA members. There are four tournaments per age group (groups include players up to 80 years of age, for women and 85 for men), each on a different surface. Singles, doubles, and mixed doubles competitions are held at facilities scattered throughout the United States. Special attractions: father-son and mother-daughter doubles events.
For information: USTA, 70 W. Red Oak Lane, White Plains, NY 10604-3602; 914-696-7000.

VAN DER MEER TENNIS UNIVERSITY

Van der Meer Tennis University offers inexpensive five-day Seniors Clinics regularly from August to May every year, most at its center on Hilton Head Island but a few in Lakeland, Florida. Specifically for 50-plus players, beginning or experienced, the clinics provide more than 16 hours of instruction, including video analysis, tactics and strategies for singles and doubles, match play drills, plus round robins, social activities, and free court time. The goal is to improve your strokes and match-play skills and show you how to get more enjoyment out of your game. Discounted accommodations are available for participants at the Players Club next door, a block from the beach. If you attend a clinic on a nonsenior week or weekend, you will get a 10 percent discount by showing your AARP card.

For information: Van der Meer Tennis University, PO Box 5902, Hilton Head Island, SC 29938-5902; 800-845-6138 (or 803-785-8388).

MORE TENNIS VACATIONS

If playing tennis is an essential part of a vacation for you, check out the offerings of the National Senior Sports Association and the Over the Hill Gang.

WALKING TOURS

There are so many organizations that offer walking/hiking trips designed for or eminently suited to mature travelers that we can't list them all here. The following, however, specialize in travel on foot. Other walking trips are mentioned throughout the book.

ELDERTREKS

On these trekking trips to exotic lands, most of them in the Far East, you will hike overland on foot and, in many cases, sleep on an air mattress in a tribal village or a tent. (For more, see Chapter 5.)

For information: ElderTreks, 597 Markham St., Toronto, ON M6G 2L7; 800-741-7956 or 416-588-5000.

HOSTELLING INTERNATIONAL/AMERICAN YOUTH HOSTELS

Several of the Discovery Tours run by HI/AYH every year are exclusively for over-50s (see Chapter 3). On these van-supported hiking trips limited to 10 vigorous, conditioned, mature adventurers, you sleep at a base camp, usually a hostel, and set forth each morning on a moderate hike carrying only your day pack and a water bottle while the van lugs the rest of your belongings.

HI/AYH membership, which is required, costs $25 per year unless you are over 55, when it is reduced to $15.

For information: HI/AYH, Dept. 855, 733 15th St. NW, Washington, DC 20005; 202-783-6161.

SENIOR WORLD TOURS

This agency plans several six-day walking tours especially geared for energetic people in their prime. One trip takes you on hikes in the Jackson Hole area in Wyoming, which includes the Tetons and Yellowstone National Park, putting you up at a mountain lodge. Another offers lodgings in historic inns and rambles through the byways, centuries-old towns, and hedgerows of the Cotswolds in England. And a third choice, among others, is a foot tour of Washington State's Olympic Peninsula, where you'll explore such sights as Mount Olympus, the Olympic rain forest, and Lake Quinault. **For information:** Senior World Tours, 3701 Buttrick Rd. SE, Ada, MI 49301-9221; 800-676-5801 or 616-676-5885.

WALK ABOUT THE WEST
Walk About the West specializes in guided walking trips exclusively for "active folks over 50," exploring places you can't see from a car or bus but sleeping in real beds at night. Its ventures take you to unique locations in the scenic West, where you hike, enjoy the sights, view the wildlife, and bunk in a motel or lodge, staying in one place from start to finish. Recent tours have included Arches and Canyonlands National Parks in Utah, the Pikes Peak region of the Colorado Rockies, Olympic National Park (Washington), Rocky Mountain National Park (Colorado), and the desert of Southeast Utah. **For information:** Walk About the West, 376C Rockrimmon Blvd., Colorado Springs, CO 80919; 719-531-9577.

WALKING THE WORLD
Anyone who loves adventure, is at least 50 years old, and is in good physical shape is invited to participate in Walking the World's explorations. These are 7- to 17-day back-country treks, covering 7 to 10 miles a day, that focus on natural and cultural history. On some trips, you'll camp out and, carrying light gear, hike to each new destination. On others, you will lodge in cabins,

small inns, or B&Bs, setting forth on daily walks into the countryside. Groups are small, from 12 to 18 participants and two guides, and there's no upper age limit.

Destinations include Canyon de Chelly and Chaco Canyon in Arizona and New Mexico, Arches and Canyonlands National Parks in Utah, Scotland, Ireland, New Zealand, Maine, Hawaii, and a llama-trekking trip (llamas carry your gear) in the San Juan Mountains of Colorado.

For information: Walking the World, PO Box 1186, Fort Collins, CO 80522; 800-340-9255 or 303-225-0500.

MOTORCYCLE HEAVEN

BEACH'S MOTORCYCLE ADVENTURES

If motorcycling is your passion and adventure is in your blood, look into the motorcycle tours offered by this agency. Founded by Bob and Elizabeth Beach, both in their 70s, it invites all ages including yours to choose between two itineraries—one for two weeks, the other for three: the Alpine Adventure, which takes you through the mountains of Germany, Austria, Italy, France, and Switzerland, or the Maori Meander, which escorts you into the backcountry of New Zealand. Although you'll get a day-by-day itinerary, the daily routing, pace, and stops are up to you. Your group will meet each evening at a prearranged hotel where you'll eat dinner and breakfast the next morning.

For information: Beach's Motorcycle Adventures, 2763 W. River Parkway, Grand Island, NY 14072-2053; 716-773-4960.

RETREADS MOTORCYCLE CLUB

Retreads are motorcycle enthusiasts who have reached the ripe old age of 40 and who get together to talk cycling mainly through correspondence. Sometimes, though, they meet at area, regional, and international rallies, with or without their bikes. If you join—there is no membership fee—a club newsletter will keep you informed of the activities going on among the 30,000 members in the U.S., Canada, and a few other countries. **For information:** Retreads Motorcycle Club International, 8749 SW 21st St., Topeka, KS 66615; 913-478-4508.

CANOE VACATIONS

ELDERHOSTEL

Some of the programs offered by Elderhostel include canoeing in their course offerings. Recently, for example, canoeing has been one of the curriculum choices for wilderness trips in Maine and Colorado.

For information: Elderhostel, 75 Federal St., Boston, MA 02110; 617-426-7788.

KAYAKING TOURS

NEW ZEALAND ADVENTURES

Here's your chance to take a five-day sea kayak tour on the other side of the world, paddling in the Bay of Islands in New Zealand. Here on this tour expressly for people over 50, you'll stay at an isolated island home set in Maritime Park, eat home-cooked meals, and, with experienced guides, spend your days exploring the volcanic rock formations and sea caves by kayak. In between you'll have time for day hikes to panoramic overlooks, swimming, snorkeling, sailing, and learning about the native culture of the Polynesian Maoris. Go in New Zealand's summer months—December through April.

For information: New Zealand Adventures, 1701 Meridian Ave. North, Seattle, WA 98113; 206-364-0160.

GOLFING VACATIONS

GREENS FEES

Most municipal and many private golf courses offer senior golfers (usually those over 65) a discount off the regular greens fees. Take your identification with you and always make inquiries before you play.

THE GOLF CARD

This card, designed especially for senior golfers with lots of time to play on every possible golf course, costs $95 the first year for a single membership or $145 for two and thereafter $85 for a single and $135 for a double per year. It entitles you to two complimentary 18-hole rounds or 50 percent off players' fees at each of nearly 3,000 member golf courses throughout the world.

Membership benefits include a Quest International card that gives you 50 percent discounts on hotels and motels, the bimonthly *Golf Traveler* magazine, which contains a directory and guide to the participating courses and resorts, and discounts at many resorts when you book golf travel packages.

The average member of this group is 61 years old and has played golf for 24 years, plays 81 rounds a year,

200

travels 11 weeks a year, travels with a spouse, and plans golf as an important part of his or her leisure travel.
For information: The Golf Card, PO Box 7020, Englewood, CO 80155; 800-321-8269 or 303-790-2267.

NSSA GOLF HOLIDAYS
The National Senior Sports Association (see the beginning of this chapter) sponsors golf holidays at highly rated courses all over the U.S. The four-day trips are scheduled once or twice a month, with the moderate cost covering fees, most meals, lodging, and cocktail parties. Golfing vacations, usually for a week or 10 days, are also planned in such golfing meccas as Scotland, Ireland, Mexico, Canada, the Caribbean, and Hawaii. Occasionally, too, you will be offered golfing cruises to the Caribbean or Bermuda, playing a few rounds instead of shopping whenever you're in port.

Golfers are paired by handicaps, with a separate division for those players without established handicaps. Activities are planned for nonplaying spouses, and solo travelers are welcomed.

When you join NSSA, you'll receive a monthly newsletter that will alert you to the latest happenings.
For information: NSSA, 167 Old Post Rd., Southport, CT 06490; 800-282-6772.

JOHN JACOBS GOLF SCHOOLS
Golfers over the age of 62 get 10 percent off the cost of a four-day or weekend package from July through December at any John Jacobs Golf School around the country. Most packages include lodging, breakfast and

dinner, instruction, greens fees, and cart for extra rounds.
For information: Call 800-472-5007.

CALYPSO 50+ WINTER GOLF SERIES

These all-inclusive, moderately priced golf packages put you up at Wyndham Rose Hall, 15 minutes from Montego Bay, Jamaica. The packages include airfare from Tampa, three meals a day, nightly entertainment, unlimited bar drinks, and water sports. More important, they feature unlimited golf greens fees, a shared cart for 18 holes daily, and one caddy per cart per day. You may stay for three nights, four nights, or a week and, if you like, take along some under-50 companions.
For information: Call your travel agent or 800-873-4423.

SWIMMING FOR FUN AND FITNESS

Swimming, a great way to get exercise and stay in shape, is, for most of us, simply a matter of jumping into the nearest lake or pool and butterflying around, maybe doing a few laps. But if you'd like to be organized about it, you'll find that many Ys and other pool operators have special swim classes or meets for adults. Or you can get really serious and join the Masters Swimmers.

U.S. MASTERS SWIMMING

Originally an organization for young competitive swimmers fresh out of college looking for people to race against, today the Masters is a group that is about 80 percent recreational swimmers, many of whom are over 50. Members get swimming insurance and receive a national newsletter and a magazine that offer information about places to swim, groups to swim with, tips on techniques, and the like. There are 54 local associations across the United States for you to hook up with and several weekend or week-long swim camps to consider.

If you're into competition, at whatever age or level of ability, you may participate in local, regional, and even national meets. Competitors are grouped in heats according to their times, regardless of age or sex. But results are tabulated separately for men and women and in five-year age groups right through 90-plus.

For information: USMS National Office, 2 Peter Ave., Rutland, MA 01543; 508-886-6631.

EVENTS FOR RAPID RUNNERS

FIFTY-PLUS FITNESS ASSOCIATION

This is not a club, although it occasionally sponsors athletic events for its over-50 members. It is an organization formed by eminent exercise researchers at Stanford University for the exchange of information about physical exercise and its benefits (and hazards) among the older population. Its members, from almost every state and several foreign countries, also serve as volunteers for ongoing studies of such activities as running, swimming, biking, and racewalking. Each is asked to contribute $20 a year, tax-deductible, to defray costs.

For information: Fifty-Plus Fitness Association, PO Box D, Stanford, CA 94309; 415-323-6160.

MASTERS RUNNING AND TRACK AND FIELD

Masters are men and women over 40 who participate in organized track and field competitions, racewalking, and long-distance running races held frequently during the year. Competition is divided by gender into five- or 10-year age groups in every event from the 100-meter dash to the shot put to the marathon. For many of the events, you simply show up at the right time and place, register, and participate. However, it is usually necessary to register in advance, and many events do not accept day-of-race registration. All competitions are open to all athletes in the designated age ranges. There are no qualifying standards, and competitors are grouped according to their individual levels.

Experienced athletes may enter regional, national, and international Masters competitions, again open to everyone, where they pay their own expenses and compete as individuals.

For continuing information about events, meet results, schedules, and local news, you may subscribe to the *National Masters News*, a monthly newspaper.

For information: USA Track and Field, 1 RCA Dome, Ste. 140, Indianapolis, IN 46225; 317-261-0500. For subscription information: *National Masters News*, PO Box 2372, Van Nuys, CA 91404.

OVER-50 SOFTBALL

**NATIONAL ASSOCIATION OF
SENIOR CITIZEN SOFTBALL**

The NASCS is an association of several thousand softball players and hundreds of teams in the U.S. and Canada,

with a goal of promoting a worldwide interest in senior softball. To play ball on one of its teams, you must be at least 50 years old. There's no upper age limit, and both men and women are welcomed. NASCS is the organizer of the annual Senior Softball World Series, a tournament for players who must first qualify in local competitions. Last year 113 teams from the U.S. and Canada competed in Orlando, Florida. A quarterly magazine keeps members up to date on happenings here and abroad.
For information: NASCS, PO Box 1085, Mt. Clemens, MI 48046; 810-792-2110.

SENIOR SOFTBALL–USA

This organization conducts softball tournaments all over the country and organizes international tournaments as well, including the Senior Softball World Championship Games held in September. Anyone over 50, man or woman, in the U.S. and Canada may join. Members get assistance finding teams in their areas and may subscribe to the *Senior Softball–USA News,* which keeps them up to date on tournaments and other news. They are eligible to take part in an annual international tour that takes teams to play ball in foreign lands.
For information: Senior Softball–USA, 9 Fleet Ct., Sacramento, CA 95831; 916-393-8566.

NATIONAL SENIOR GAMES

U.S. NATIONAL SENIOR SPORTS ORGANIZATION

The USNSO is a not-for-profit organization, sponsored by major corporations, that promotes health and fitness for seniors through competitive multisport events across the country, including the U.S. Senior Sports Classic, the Senior Olympics. This event occurs every two years.

To qualify for the more than 500 separate events—in track and field, swimming, cycling, golf, tennis, bowling, volleyball, horseshoes, archery, 5- and 10-kilometer runs, badminton, softball, racquetball, racewalking, 3-on-3 basketball, triathlon, shuffleboard, and table tennis—athletes must first qualify in authorized state competitions across the country. The events are organized for men and women in five-year age brackets from 55 to 100-plus.

If you want to be ready to go for the next senior games, get the ground rules from your local senior sports organization or the national headquarters.

For information: U.S. National Senior Sports Organization, 14323 S. Outer Forty Rd., Ste. N300, Chesterfield, MO 63017; 314-878-4900.

INTERNATIONAL GAMES

INTERNATIONAL SENIOR GAMES
Scheduled to debut in April 1996 and then to be held every three years in Bermuda, the 15-day International Senior Games invites athletes at least 50 years old to participate in 20 different sports as well as four cultural activities such as storytelling and creative writing. Participants, divided into different age groups, may join either of two levels of competition: the Elite Class, reserved for those who have achieved Olympic, professional, or all-American status, or the Masters Program, for amateur athletes who have competed regionally or locally.

In addition to the sports events at the International Senior Games, Mount Sinai Medical Center in New York will conduct medical research relating to the health of senior athletes and establish an international research program for the over-50 population.

For information: International Senior Games, 460 Summer St., Stamford, CT 06901; 800-223-6106 or 203-352-0532.

STATE SENIOR GAMES

Many states hold their own senior games once a year or so and send their best competitors to national events. If you don't find your state among those listed here, that doesn't mean there's no program in your area—many are sponsored by counties, cities, even local agencies and colleges. Check with your local city, county, or state recreation department to see what's going on near you. You don't have to be a serious competitor to enter these games but merely ready to enjoy yourself. So what if you don't go home with a medal? At the very least, you'll meet other energetic people and have a lot of laughs.

CALIFORNIA

Hundreds of senior athletes from all over the United States and Canada compete every winter in the annual California Senior Olympics–Palm Springs. The sporting events range from track and field to golf and tennis, with medal winners going on to compete in the National Senior Olympics. If you are 50 or more, a resident or a visitor to the state, you are eligible to participate.

For information: California Senior Olympics–Palm Springs, Mizell Senior Center, 480 S. Sunrise Way, Palm Springs, CA 92262; 619-323-5689.

COLORADO
The Senior Winter Games at the Summit take place each year during three days in the second week of February in the village of Breckenridge. Anyone from anywhere who's over 55 and wants to compete against his or her peers is welcome. Events include cross-country skiing, downhill slalom, speed skating, snowshoe races, biathlon, figure skating, and more, plus social activities. Age categories for the competitions begin at 55 to 59 and increase in five-year increments to 90 plus. A registration fee that allows participation in as many events as you wish currently stands at $15.

For information: Senior Winter Games at the Summit, PO Box 442, Breckenridge, CO 80424; 303-668-5486.

CONNECTICUT
The Connecticut Senior Olympics include not only competitive sport events but also a mini health fair and physical fitness activities. Connecticut residents and those from neighboring states who are 55-plus converge on the University of Bridgeport on the first weekend in June for three days of events such as the 5,000-meter run, the 100-yard dash, the mile run, the long jump, diving, bocci, and tennis. There is a $10 entrance fee.

In September, join the Connecticut Senior Olympics Sunfish Regatta, which features sailing races on Long Island Sound. Entrance fee is $20. In October, it's the

10-kilometer run/racewalk at the University of Bridge-port. Entrance fee is $5. And in March, the winter games feature downhill, giant slalom, cross-country, and snowshoe races. Again, you must be over 55 to partici-pate. Entrance fee is $30.

For information: Connecticut Senior Olympics, Harvey Hubbell Gymnasium, University of Bridgeport, Bridge-port, CT 06601; 203-576-4722.

FLORIDA

The Golden Age Games in Sanford are the biggest and the oldest Senior Games in the country. Held annually in November, they go on for a week and include plenty of competitions, ceremonies, social events, and entertain-ments. If you are over 55, you are eligible to participate regardless of residency. In other words, you needn't be a Florida resident to compete for the gold, silver, and bronze medals in such sports as basketball, biking, bowling, canoeing, checkers, diving, dance, swimming, tennis, triathlon, track and field, canasta, and croquet. There is a small entry fee for each event.

For information: The Greater Sanford Chamber of Commerce, 400 E. 1st St., Sanford, FL 32771-0868; 407-322-2212.

Palm Beach also has big games every year. Called the U.S. Senior Athletic Games, they are open to anyone 50 or older and feature competitions in everything from biking to archery, golf, shuffleboard, basketball, swim-ming, tennis, running and walking races, and track and field events. Registration is $5 for the first event and $3 for each additional competitive event. You will compete within your own five-year age range.

For information: U.S. Senior Athletic Games, 200 Castlewood Dr., North Palm Beach, FL 33408; 407-842-3030.

MICHIGAN
Michigan Senior Olympics, a four-day happening open to people 55 and older, are held every year on the campus of a state college. For small registration and event fees, you get a chance to compete for medals in athletic events from archery to volleyball. You may also take home ribbons for your baking skills, arts and crafts, and dancing. Spectators are welcomed too.
For information: Michigan Senior Olympics, 312 Woodward, Rochester, MI 48307; 810-656-1403.

MISSOURI
The St. Louis Senior Olympics have become an institution in Missouri by now. A four-day event that is open to anyone who lives anywhere and is 55 years old, it costs a nominal amount and is action-oriented. No knitting contests here—only energetic events such as bicycle races, 200-meter races, standing long jumps, tennis singles and doubles, and swimming.
For information: Senior Olympics, JCCA, 2 Millstone Campus, St. Louis, MO 63146; 314-432-5700.

MONTANA
The Big Sky State Games are held each July in Billings, again for people over 55.
For information: The Big Sky Games, PO Box 2318, Billings, MT 59101.

NEW HAMPSHIRE

For three days in September, you can compete with your peers in the Granite State Senior Summer Games, which feature 15 sports events ranging from swimming to tennis, track and field, shuffleboard, and table tennis. In alternate years, these are qualifying games for the U.S. Senior Sports Classic. Sign up if you are at least 55 and in good operating condition. The cost is minimal. Regional games are also scheduled throughout the state during the summer.

The Granite State Senior Winter Games, held in Waterville Valley for three days in March, are open to men and women 55 and over who compete in groups of five-year increments. They get a chance to challenge their peers in dual slalom, giant slalom, and cross-country races. Other events include speed skating, snowball throw, hockey goal shoot, and snowshoe races. Everyone in the appropriate age range is welcome to enter the competitions and attend both an opening reception and an awards banquet. Costs for entry, lift tickets, fees, rentals, and social affairs are low. Inexpensive lodging is also available.

For information: Larry Flint, Granite State Senior Winter Games, PO Box 942, Newport, NH 03773; 603-863-6397.

NEW YORK

The New York State Parks Senior Games are an organized sports and leisure program for state residents 55 years of age and older. Men and women compete over a four-day period in recreational and competitive divisions and choose from 40 sports, activities, drop-in events, and clinics. Entertainment, exhibits, a Celebration of the Athletes, and a dinner dance are also offered. The Senior Games are held at the State University College at Cortland, usually over a weekend in early June.

For information: New York State Parks Senior Games, Agency 1, 12th Fl., Albany, NY 12238; 518-474-3748.

NORTH CAROLINA

After local games are held statewide, the winners travel to Raleigh for the North Carolina Senior Games State Finals and, perhaps, on to the national games. Most sports are on the agenda, plus an arts competition that celebrates artists in heritage, literary, performing, and visual arts. The state also sponsors the SilverStriders, a walking club for those 50 or better that gives its members log books for tracking progress, gifts and awards, and an annual report of progress and accomplishments.

For information: North Carolina Senior Games, PO Box 33590, Raleigh, NC 27636; 919-851-5456. Silver-Striders, PO Box 33514, Raleigh, NC 27636; 919-851-5456.

PENNSYLVANIA

The Pennsylvania Senior Games "combine sports, recreation, and entertainment with fellowship." You can get some of each if you are a Pennsylvania resident who is 55 or older. The games are held over five days at a university campus where you can get lodging and three meals a day at low cost. If you prefer to stay in a motel, you'll get a senior discount.

For information: Pennsylvania Senior Games, 31 S. Hancock St., Wilkes Barre, PA 18702; 717-823-3164.

VERMONT

The Green Mountain Senior Summer Games at Green Mountain College in Poultney require you to be a Vermont resident who is over 55 and an amateur at your sport. For a $12 registration fee, you play, eat lunch, and have fun. Competitive events—organized in age groups of 55 to 62, 63 to 70, and 71 and over—include everything from golf and tennis to swimming, darts, horseshoes, walking, running, table tennis, bowling, croquet, softball, and shuffleboard. Just for fun, there are scenic walks, socials, and free swims. The games are held in September.

The Green Mountain Senior Winter Games, which take place in January, include both downhill and slalom races. The Cross-Country Senior Winter Games are held in February and include ski, snowball, and snowshoe competitions.

For information: Green Mountain Senior Games, 131 Holden Hill Rd., Weston, VT 05161; 802-824-6521.

VIRGINIA

Virginia's Golden Olympics are an annual four-day event held each spring on a college campus, this year at the College of William and Mary, in Williamsburg, where older athletes compete to qualify for the U.S. National Senior Olympics—or just for the fun of it. It is a combination of social events and entertainment with sports competitions, open to Virginia residents over the age of 55. Spouses are invited to come along and enjoy the hospitality, which includes parties, dances, tours of local sites, and other festivities. The fees are low, lodging and meals are cheap, and the sporting events are many, ranging from rope jumping, miniature golf, and riflery to swimming, running, and tennis for age groups from 55 to 85-plus.

For information: Golden Olympics, Virginia Recreation and Parks Society, Route 4, PO Box 155, Mechanicsville, VA 23111; 804-730-9447.

Chapter Fourteen
Adventures on Skis

OVER THE TOP ON TWO NARROW BOARDS

Downhill skiing is one sport you'd think would appeal only to less mature, less wise, less breakable people. On the contrary, there is an astounding number of ardent over-50 skiers who would much rather glide down mountains than sit around waiting for springtime. In fact, many of us ski more than ever now that we're older because we can go midweek when the crowds are thinner and we get impressive discounts on lift tickets. And many of us are taking up the sport for the first time. Ski schools all over the United States and Canada are reporting an increase of older students in beginner classes.

The truth is, skiing is one sport you're never too old to learn or to practice. Once you get the hang of it, you can ski at your own speed, choosing the terrain, the difficulty level, and the challenge. You can swoop down cliffs through narrow icy passes or wend your way down gentle slopes in a more leisurely fashion, aided by the new improved skis and boots, clearly marked and carefully groomed trails, and sophisticated lifts that take all the work out of getting up the mountain.

Besides, ski resorts are falling all over themselves to lure older skiers to their slopes, offering discounts, free passes, and other engaging incentives. Many over-50 groups sponsor ski activities as well.

CLUBS FOR MATURE SKIERS

"IT'S NEVER TOO LATE," PARK CITY

This program is designed to teach older beginners to ski, with specially tailored instructions for those who considered themselves too far over the hill to learn to glide down mountains gracefully. The two-hour group lessons (currently $35 per session) taught by veteran ski instructors at Park City's Ski Area in Utah are available for over-50s (and younger friends) Monday through Friday from noon to 2 P.M.

For information: "It's Never Too Late," Park City Ski Area, Box 39, Park City, UT 84060; 800-227-2754 or 801-649-8111.

IT'SNOWONDER CLUB AT SMUGGLERS' NOTCH

This club for skiers over the age of 55 meets on Wednesdays for breakfast and gets out on the slopes from 10 in the morning until 3 P.M., skiing together with a guide. A fee of $25 a day gets you lift tickets and club activities. You may attend a ski clinic for only $10 more.

For information: Smugglers' Notch Resort, Smugglers' Notch, VT 05464; 800-451-8752.

THE OVER THE HILL GANG

As we have noted, this group originated with a group of older skiers who wanted companionship on the slopes, and skiing is still its main emphasis. In fact, its motto is "Once you're over the hill, you pick up speed!"

If you are 50, you are eligible to join (your spouse may be younger) and set forth on ski adventures—both downhill and cross-country—in this country and abroad. Members get discounts on lifts and rentals and sometimes are the recipients of free group guides and special lift-line privileges. People who have never put on a pair of ski boots or haven't tried them in years can take advantage of a Learn to Ski program, refresher clinics, or group lessons arranged by the club.

And when the ski season ends, you can join the Gang for a bike trip, a party, maybe rafting or ballooning or a sailing trip in the Caribbean. This club, with an age range of 50 to 94 and an average age of 63, is definitely out for a good time.

Every year the club organizes several Senior Ski Weeks in the Rockies, Europe, Canada, and New Zealand. Future plans include the South American ski resorts. The event packages include transportation, accommodations, discounted (or free) lift tickets, parties, food, and, in some cases, ski escorts and lessons.

The local Gangs also run their own ski trips both in their own vicinities and elsewhere in the world, and all members everywhere are invited to go along. At some ski areas, members meet once a week to ski the slopes together. At Breckenridge, in Colorado, for example, local and visiting members gather every Tuesday to ski all day with their own guides and get together for lunch and après-ski. At Keystone, it's every Thursday morning during the ski season, and at Vail, Friday is the regular day for camaraderie.

Membership in the national organization costs $37

($60 for couples) plus chapter dues if a chapter is located in your area. A quarterly magazine brings you news of the club's events. An important benefit is that members (who need be only 50 to join) will get discounts similar to those offered to skiers over 65 on lift tickets, rentals, lessons, and packages at many ski areas, even when they ski on their own. Be prepared to show your OTHG membership card and a proof of identity.

For information: Over the Hill Gang International, 3310 Cedar Heights Dr., Colorado Springs, CO 80904; 719-685-4656.

MT. CRANMORE HERITAGE SKI CLUB

Every Friday morning for 10 weeks, the Heritage Ski Club meets at Mt. Cranmore, in New Hampshire, for a group lesson. You qualify if you are over 60. The cost is $125 plus your lift tickets, which are $14 midweek at age 60 and free at 70.

For information: Call 800-786-6754 or 603-356-5544.

SENIOR SKIER NETWORK

A group of 47 major ski resorts on the East Coast has joined together to host a midweek senior skier program. Each host mountain welcomes everybody over 50 to its full-day program, which includes clinics and ski instruction with four hours of on-snow lessons and other activities that vary from mountain to mountain. Cost is more than a lift ticket but less than a lift/lesson combination. Many of these areas also offer a Senior Program Package for the season. Each area's program feeds into the winter state games in Vermont, Connecticut, Massachusetts, and New York.

For information: Eastern Professional Ski Instructors Assn., 1-A Lincoln Ave., Albany, NY 12205-4900; 518-452-6095.

70+ SKI CLUB

You must prove you are 70 before you can join this club that now has almost 10,000 members, all of them in their 70s, 80s, and 90s as well as one active member who's 103. The club meets at ski areas for races, companionship, and partying and organizes big trips in the U.S. and other parts of the world.

Lloyd T. Lambert, a former ski columnist who was born in 1901, founded the 70+ Ski Club in 1977 with 34 members. Its main purpose was to make skiing less expensive for older people on limited incomes, and the campaign worked. Today most ski areas give over-70s free or half-price lift tickets. Says Lambert, "We provide inspiration to the 50-year-olds who consider themselves too old and feeble to ski."

Hunter Mountain, in New York's Catskills, hosts the club's annual meeting every year in early March. This is when the 70+ Ski Races are held, an event so popular that the contestants are divided into three age groups: men 70 to 80, women 70 to 80, and everyone over 80. There are serious slalom races with awards presented at a gala party at the lodge.

Most gatherings of the members take place in New York state and New England, but there are always at least a couple of longer trips to the Alps, the Rockies, or even to Australia, New Zealand, and Argentina. The club has members in all parts of the United States and Canada as well as Europe.

Lifetime membership costs $5 ($15 if you live outside of the U.S.). Proof of your date of birth is required with your application, and you may not apply more than two weeks before your 70th birthday. You will receive a 70+ Ski Club patch, a newsletter that tells you about upcoming events, and a list of ski areas where you can ski free or at substantial discounts.
For information: Lloyd T. Lambert, 70+ Ski Club, 104 Eastside Dr., Ballston Lake, NY 12019; 518-399-5458.

SILVER PEAKS
Any intrepid skier who is over the age of 50 is invited to join the Silver Peaks, a group that skis together every Tuesday at Jay Peak, in Vermont, for fun and instruction. Membership is free. After complimentary coffee and donuts in the morning, you ski in compatible groups guided by instructors, stopping for lunch and an après-ski gathering.
For information: Call Jay Peak, 802-988-2611.

SKI WINDHAM SENIOR DEVELOPMENT PROGRAM
Skiers over 50 are invited to join the Senior Skier Development Program for seven or 10 consecutive Tuesdays. You get daily lift tickets, four hours of instruction, continental breakfast, workshops, videotaping, and lectures on skiing and healthy living.
For information: Ski Windham, PO Box 459, Windham, NY 12496; 800-729-7549 or 518-734-5070.

SUNDAY RIVER'S PRIME TIME SKI CLUB

A club for skiers over 50, Prime Time meets Tuesdays and Thursdays from 10 A.M. to noon and includes lift ticket and instruction for $30 a day.

For information: Sunday River, PO Box 450, Bethel, ME 04217; 800-543-2754.

WATERVILLE VALLEY SILVER STREAKS

The Silver Streaks of Waterville Valley, New Hampshire, are members of a free club for skiers who have reached their 55th birthday (and spouses at any age). What you get Mondays through Thursdays are reserved parking, free coffee and donuts, social events, occasional seminars on subjects ranging from ski tuning to financial planning, a five-day racing camp, race clinics, warm-up runs with the staff, and Silver Streak NASTAR races. Membership also entitles you to reduced prices on rentals and class lessons and a one-third reduction on lodging, also midweek.

For beginners over 55, the resort offers a learn-to-ski package with lifts, ski lesson, and rental equipment.

Skiers 60 through 69 ski here at junior rates. But members of the 70+ Ski Club—and any other skiers over the age of 70—ski free midweek except on holidays. They also may participate in challenge races and instruction clinics during the season.

For information: Waterville Valley Silver Streaks, Waterville Valley, NH 03215; 800-468-2553 or 603-236-8311.

THE WILD OLD BUNCH

This merry band of senior skiers who navigate the steep slopes of Alta in Utah is an informal group of men and women from Utah and many other states who ski together for fun, welcoming anybody who wants to join them. There are no rules, no designated leaders, no lessons, no regular meetings, and no age restrictions, though most members are well past 50, retired business or professional people. Somewhere between 50 and 100 avid skiers now wear the Wild Old Bunch patch.

The group grows haphazardly as members pick up stray mature skiers they find on the slopes, showing them their mountain and passing along their enthusiasm for the steeper trails and the off-trail skiing in Alta's famous powder. Says a spokesperson, Rush Spedden, "If you visit Alta and would like to join in some of the old-fashioned camaraderie of skiing, just look for any of us on the slopes or on the deck of the mid-mountain Alpenglow Inn, where we gather for lunch and tales. Either ski with us or grab a seat for some lively conversation."

Although the bunch isn't sexist, some of the wives prefer to stay on less difficult slopes or to travel the cross-country trails, so they wear "Wild Wives" patches. **For information:** Look for the Wild Old Bunch on the slopes.

MORE GOOD DEALS FOR DOWNHILL SKIERS

The older you are, the less it costs to ski. There's hardly a ski area in North America today that doesn't give mature skiers a good deal. Many cut the price of lift tickets in half at age 60, others do so at 65, and most stop charging altogether at 70. Some make offers on season passes that are hard to refuse. And others plan special senior programs specifically for mature skiers.

To give you an idea of what's out there, here is a sampling of the possibilities. It does not include all areas, of course, so be sure to check out others in locations that interest you. Carry proof of age with you at all times.

ARIZONA
Mature skiers over 62 ski for $10 a day, a third of the regular adult rates at Sunrise Park Resort. Over-70 skiers pay nothing for their lift tickets.

CALIFORNIA
Among the ski areas in California that give senior skiers good deals on lift tickets are Mammoth Mountain, where you get a discount at 65; Alpine Meadows, discounted rates over 65, no charge at 70; Badger Pass, no charge over 65; Iron Mountain, discounted lift tickets at 65 and special lessons and packages. Tahoe Donner charges a reduced fee at 60 and nothing at 70. Northstar, at Tahoe, charges half at 60. Its free one-hour Senior Clinics are offered every Wednesday to skiers over 60 as well as three-day clinics for intermediate senior skiers. At Squaw Valley, lift tickets cost only $5 for skiers over the age of 65. At Boreal, if you're over 60 you pay just $10 a day; over 70, you pay nothing.

COLORADO
The ski areas offering discounted senior lift tickets, some starting at 60 and many charging nothing at 70,

include Arapahoe Basin, Arrowhead, Aspen Highlands, Aspen Mountain, Beaver Creek, Berthoud Pass, Breckenridge, Buttermilk, Copper Mountain, Crested Butte, Eldora Mountain, Keystone, Loveland, Monarch, Powderhorn, Purgatory, Silver Creek, Ski Cooper, Ski Sunlight, Snowmass, Steamboat, Telluride, Vail, Winter Park, and Wolf Creek. In fact, as you can see, it's a rare ski area that has no senior discounts.

In addition, a few areas have instituted special senior ski programs. For example, Steamboat's Come Smell the Roses program caters to skiers over 45 with daily lessons. And Over the Hill Gang members meet to ski together four days a week. At Keystone, one day a week is designated Senior Day, when you may learn to ski or improve your skills with special lessons.

IDAHO

Skiers 65 and over get a discount at the country's first big ski resort, at Sun Valley. Check out Sun Valley's Prime Time week in January, with special rates, instruction, races, and festivities exclusively for skiers over 60.

MAINE

Sunday River Ski Resort not only reduces lift costs but has its own over-50 club. Sugarloaf/USA cuts lift tickets and season passes almost in half for skiers over 65. Other areas with reduced tickets and other perks for older skiers include Shawnee Peak and Saddleback.

MICHIGAN

At Crystal Mountain, skiers over 55 get half-price lift

tickets, lessons, and rentals. Shanty Creek–Schuss Mountain also reduces its rates at 55.

More than 30 ski areas all over Michigan now offer a February week of free lift tickets and/or lessons for skiers over 60.

NEVADA

Lift tickets at Mt. Rose and Diamond Peak are reduced if you're over 60. At Ski Incline, every Wednesday is Senior Social Day for over-55s, when for a small fee, you get skiing, morning coffee, brunch, and speakers.

NEW HAMPSHIRE

Look for a good deal on lift tickets at Loon Mountain, where skiers over 65 pay about half for season passes and those over 70 don't pay a cent. Waterville Valley cuts the rate back to junior rates at 65 and allows free skiing at 70 midweek. At Mt. Cranmore, you take $5 off at 60, and at 70 you ski for $5 any time including weekends. Other good deals may be found at Bretton Woods, Dartmouth, Attitash, Black Mountain, and Wildcat. TGIF ("Thank Goodness I'm Fifty") at Attitash meets every Thursday for group skiing.

NEW MEXICO

Santa Fe offers skiers over 62 a third off on lift tickets while over-70s ski free. To ski at Taos, it's less than half for those over 65 and free at 70. And at Angel Fire, those over 65 ski free.

NEW YORK

At Gore Mountain, you'll get the junior rate if you're

over 62 and ski free if you're over 70. The same good
deal is available at Ski Windham but starting at 65.
Other areas that discount the lift tickets at 62 include
Catamount, Greek Peak, and Belleayre. Hunter starts at
65, Sterling Forest at 55, and most areas allow you to ski
free at 70.

PENNSYLVANIA
Discounted lift tickets are yours at Camelback, Blue
Marsh, and Hidden Valley, among others, in this state.
Eagle Rock cuts the price at age 50.

UTAH
Park City and Snow Basin offer half-price lift tickets to
people who have made it past 65. The lifts are reduced at
62 at Snowbird and are free at Park City, Snowbird,
Solitude, and Sundance for those over 70. At Alta, older
skiers pay junior rates and nothing after 80.

VERMONT
Vermont's ski areas are old hands at discounts for mature skiers. Among them:
    Ascutney: Skiers 65 to 69 pay junior rates for lift
tickets, while those over 70 ski free.
    Bolton Valley: Those 65 to 69 ski at junior rates. Se-
niors 70 and over ski free.
    Bromley: Skiers 65 and over pay only $15 for a mid-
week lift ticket. On weekends and holidays, over-70s ski
free, while those 65 to 69 pay half price. Every Tuesday,
the Silver Griffins, a club for seniors, meets for an unstructured day of camaraderie and skiing.
    Burke Mountain: If you're over 65 you pay the junior

rate any day; Super Seniors (over 75) ski free. All may join the Senior Skier Tuneup, a two-hour session with a peer instructor for a modest fee.

Haystack: Skiers over 65 pay junior rates.

Jay Peak: Here you pay only $5 for a lift ticket if you are 65. The Silver Peaks Club, for skiers over 50, meets every Tuesday.

Killington: You pay the junior rates for lifts, rentals, and ski school if you are over 65.

Middlebury College Snow Bowl: Skiers 62 through 69 ski at the student rate any day or may purchase a season pass at a reduced rate. Those over 70 get a free lifetime pass.

Okemo Mountain: From 65 to 69, you pay junior rates for lift tickets and group lessons. If you're 70 or over, you get a season ticket at a bargain price.

Pico Ski Resort: Anyone over 65 pays half price, while a skier over 70 skis free.

Smuggler's Notch Resort: At 65, you get a good deal on lift tickets. At 70, you ski free. The It'SnoWonder Club, which is free for skiers over 55, meets every Wednesday to ski together and socialize all day.

Stowe Mountain Resort: Over-65s may purchase season passes or day tickets at the junior rate. A Super Seniors Card is available to 70-plus skiers, which allows them to ski Sunday through Thursday at a greatly reduced rate.

Stratton Mountain: Skiers aged 62 to 69 pay the junior rate. Over-70 skiers ski for even lower rates.

Sugarbush Resort: At 65 to 69, you ski at a discounted rate, while over-70s ski free any day.

Suicide Six: Skiers over 65 get lift tickets at the junior rate.

VIRGINIA

Massanutten Ski Resort gives reduced rates at 65, as does Bryce. Wintergreen starts at 60.

WASHINGTON

In Washington state, many ski areas give senior discounts. Among them are Crystal Mountain, Alpental, Mission Ridge, Stevens Pass, and White Pass.

WISCONSIN

Here, the discounts are to be found at Mt. Ashwabay, Crystal Ridge, Cascade Mountain, Wintergreen, Trollhaugen, and Tyrol Basin, among others. Some even start cutting the prices at age 55.

WYOMING

At the Jackson Hole Resort, seniors over 65 ski for junior rates. At Grand Targhee Resort in Alta, those 62 to 69 ski for junior rates, while the over-70s ski free. At Snow King Resort in Jackson, it's the junior rate for skiers 60 or over.

OTHER ALPINE ADVENTURES

SENIOR WINTER GAMES AT THE SUMMIT

Here's where you can participate in multisport winter games specifically for people 55 and over. Usually held the second week in February at Breckenridge, Colorado, an old Victorian town, the event invites anybody who wants to compete. It includes downhill ski racing, cross-country ski racing, relays, a biathlon, a snowshoe race, ice speed skating, figure skating, a snowball throw, and a hockey goal shoot. The $15 entry fee allows you to enter as many of the events as you like.

For information: Senior Winter Games at the Summit, PO Box 442, Breckenridge, CO 80424; 303-668-5486.

SKI NEW ZEALAND

Eight times a year, Ski New Zealand plans ski trips to this faraway country in the Southern Hemisphere especially for over-50s (and younger companions). Scheduled in our summer months—New Zealand's winter—the 14-day packages take you to seven different resorts in New Zealand's Southern Alps. The packages include airfare from Los Angeles, accommodations, ground transportation, free lift tickets for over-50s, free stopovers, and sightseeing. Sign up early and you may stop over in Australia, Tahiti, Fiji, or Hawaii.

For information: Ski New Zealand, 150 Powell St., San Francisco, CA 94102; 800-822-5494 or 415-421-3171.

SKIING WITH ELDERHOSTEL

Many Elderhostel programs hosted by colleges and other institutions offer week-long downhill (and cross-country) learn-to-ski or intermediate programs for people over the age of 55 (and their younger companions). Just like other Elderhostel adventures, they are relatively inexpensive and always combine the skiing with lectures and classes, lodging, and meals. All are listed in the voluminous catalogs sent out regularly by this organization.

For information: Elderhostel, 75 Federal St., Boston, MA 02110; 617-426-7788.

DOWNHILL RACES FOR ALL AGES (INCLUDING YOURS)

NASTAR

NASTAR (National Standard Race) is a recreational race program for downhill skiers regardless of age, with races held in ski areas all over the United States for medals based on age, sex, and handicap. The age divisions that apply to *you* are the following: men/women 50 to 59, men/women 60 to 69, men 70 to 79, women 70 and over, and men 80 and over. You may race on your own, competing against friends and family, or as part of a participating ski club.

To join in the fun, you must complete a registration and release form at any participating NASTAR ski area. You may race as many times as you like, but only your best handicap of the day is recorded and could win you a medal for that day if you qualify as a winner in your category. A low handicap may qualify you for a national or state rankings placement.

For information: NASTAR, 402-D, AABC, Aspen, CO 81611; 303-925-7864.

CROSS-COUNTRY SKI ADVENTURES

Many cross-country areas also give senior skiers a break. Always ask about discounts before paying admission, because you may save a few of your hard-earned dollars.

CROSS-COUNTRY SKI TRIPS FOR WOMEN

Check out this agency (see Chapter 3) for cross-country skiing adventures with instruction to such locations as Minnesota near the Canadian border (five days) and Yosemite National Park (seven days). For women who live near Boston, there are weekend trips to nearby ski resorts such as Stowe, Vermont.

For information: Outdoor Vacations for Women Over 40, PO Box 200, Groton, MA 01450; 508-448-3331.

ELDERHOSTEL

Elderhostel, known for its low-cost learning vacations for people over 55 (and companions who may be younger) at educational institutions (see Chapter 16), has combined cross-country skiing and winter nature exploration since 1978. Since the programs change from year to year, you must check out the offerings in its catalogs.

For information: Elderhostel, 75 Federal St., Boston, MA 02110; 617-426-7788.

WATERVILLE VALLEY

Cross-country skiers may join Waterville Valley Silver Streaks Club if they are over 55, applying the membership benefits to the resort's 100-kilometer cross-country center. See Waterville Valley Silver Streaks in this chapter for details.

For information: Waterville Valley, NH 03215; 603-236-8311.

FOR SNOWMOBILE ENTHUSIASTS

SENIOR WORLD TOURS

This agency, formerly known as Sno-World Snow Tours, specializes in winter adventures exclusively for snow lovers over 50. Its six-day trips, based at Togwotee Mountain Lodge, 50 miles out of Jackson Hole, Wyoming, give you three days of snowmobiling (snowmobile suits with boots and helmets included), a visit to Yellowstone National Park, and a trip to Jackson that includes a sleigh ride through the National Elk Refuge. No snowmobile experience is required, but you should be in good physical shape.

For information: Senior World Tours, 3701 Buttrick Rd. SE, Ada, MI 49301-9221; 800-676-5801 or 616-676-5885.

Chapter Fifteen
Back to Summer Camp

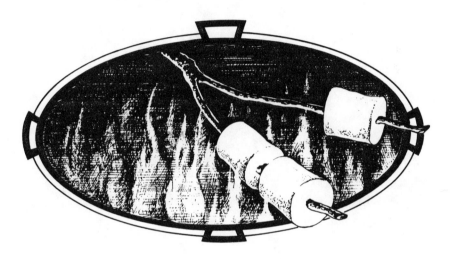

M aybe you thought camp was just for kids, but if you are a grown-up person who likes the outdoors, swimming, boating, birds, and arts and crafts and who appreciates fields and forests and star-filled skies, you too can pack your bags and go off on a sleepaway. Throughout the country, many camps set aside weeks for adult sessions, while others offer adult programs all season long. More and more adults are getting hooked on summer camp, and many wouldn't miss a year.

ELDERHOSTEL
Many of Elderhostel's programs are a combination of camping and college. In this wildly successful low-cost educational program (see Chapter 16 for details), you can spend a week or two camping in remote scenic areas, enjoying all the activities from horseback riding to crafts, boating, campfires, and sleeping in a cabin or under the stars.

For information: Elderhostel, 75 Federal St., Boston, MA 02110; 617-426-7788. In Canada: Elderhostel Canada, 308 Wellington St., Kingston, ON K7K 7A7; 613-530-2222.

RV ELDERHOSTELS

Less expensive than regular Elderhostel programs because you take along your own housing, these programs come in two varieties. One is the usual Elderhostel educational vacation on a college campus, where you partake of the happenings, including courses, meals, and excursions, with the rest of the group but sleep in your own RV, trailer, or tent on the campus or at nearby campgrounds. The other is a mobile program or moving field trip—in Alaska, for example, Wyoming, the Yukon, or along the Oregon Trail—where you'll hear the lectures over your CB radio as you travel. Moving along like a wagon train, you travel in a group led by an experienced guide and make many stops for lectures and sightseeing as you go.

For information: Elderhostel, 75 Federal St., Boston, MA 02110; 617-426-7788. In Canada: Elderhostel Canada, 308 Wellington St., Kingston, ON K7K 7A7; 613-530-2222.

GRANDPARENTS/GRANDCHILDREN CAMP

See Chapter 3 for information about summer camps and other vacations designed to give grandparents and grandchildren some special time together.

INTERHOSTEL

Sponsored by the University of New Hampshire, Interhostel offers programs that combine travel and study while you live on college campuses or in modest hotels for at least two weeks at a time (see Chapter 16). Always in foreign countries, its trips are inexpensive and packed with learning opportunities.

For information: Interhostel, University of New Hampshire, 6 Garrison Ave., Durham, NH 03824; 800-733-9753.

THE SALVATION ARMY
The Salvation Army operates 55 rural camps across the country, most of which have year-round adult sessions. The camps are run by regional divisional headquarters of the Army; thus, each is totally different from the others. Open to anyone, they cost very little.
For information: Contact a local unit of the Salvation Army.

VOLUNTARY ASSOCIATION FOR SENIOR CITIZEN ACTIVITIES
VASCA is a nonprofit organization that will provide you with detailed information about camps in the New York area for people over the age of 55. It represents 11 vacation lodges scattered about New York, New Jersey, Connecticut, and Pennsylvania, all of them amazingly affordable. Some are small rustic country retreats, most are lakeside resorts, some are huge sprawling complexes with endless activities. Several are designed to accommodate the disabled and the blind as well as the very elderly. The camps are sponsored by various nonprofit organizations and foundations, some with religious affiliations but nonsectarian.
For information: VASCA, 275 Seventh Ave., New York, NY 10001; 212-645-6590.

YMCA/YWCA
The Y runs many camps, most of them for children, but with special sessions for adults over 50. For example,

Westwind on the Pacific is a 500-acre camp owned by the Portland, Oregon, YWCA and located on the coast at the mouth of the Salmon River Estuary. Its senior week, for people over 55, is held every August and costs about $100 for everything. Camp Cheerio, run by the High Point, North Carolina, YMCA, is in the Appalachian Mountains and sets aside three weeks a year for campers over 50, who live in the same cabins and pursue all the same activities as the kids do during the rest of the summer.

For information: Ask your local YMCA or YWCA for information about camps in your area.

CAMPS SPONSORED BY CHURCH GROUPS

There are many camps and summer workshops sponsored by religious organizations, too many and too diverse to list here. One source of information is Christian Camping International, which offers four low-cost regional guides to camps in the U.S.

For information: Christian Camping International/ USA, PO Box 62189, Colorado Springs, CO 80962-2189; 719-260-9400.

AUDUBON ECOLOGY CAMPS

Not for over-50s alone, these are included here because mature nature lovers will enjoy these natural-history programs for adults run by the National Audubon Society. There are three Audubon Ecology Camps for grown-ups (in Wyoming, Maine, and Connecticut) where the outdoors is used as a classroom for six-day sessions during the summer months. Here you live on-site while you learn all about the surrounding environment, from marine and island ecology to mountain, meadow, woods, and water habitats.

For information: National Audubon Society, 613 Riversville Rd., Greenwich, CT 06831; 203-869-2017.

Chapter Sixteen

Going Back to School After 50

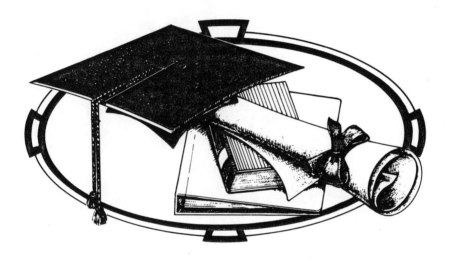

Have you always wanted to learn French, study African birds, examine Eskimo culture, delve into archaeology, international finance, horticulture, the language of whales, or great literature of the 19th century? Now is the time to do it. If you're a typical member of the over-50 generation, you're in good shape, healthy and alert, with the energy and the time to pursue new interests. So why not go back to school and learn all those things you've always wished you knew?

You are welcome as a regular student at just about any institution in the United States and Canada, especially in the continuing-education programs, but many colleges and universities have set up special programs designed to lure older people back to the classroom. Some offer good reductions in tuition (so good indeed that sometimes you may attend regular classes half price or even free) and give credits for life experience. Others have designed programs, and sometimes whole schools, specifically for mature scholars.

Going back to class is an excellent way to generate feelings of accomplishment and to exercise the mind—and one of the best ways to make new friends. It doesn't necessarily mean you'll have to turn in term papers or take excruciatingly difficult exams. Sign up for one class a week on flower arranging or Spanish conversation or a once-a-month lecture series on managing your money. Or register as a part-time or full-time student in a traditional university program. Or take a learning vacation on a college campus. Do it *your* way.

You don't even have to attend classes to learn on vacation. You can go on archaeological digs, count butterflies, help save turtles from extinction, brush up on your bassoon playing, listen to opera, search for Roman remains in Europe, study dancing or French cuisine, or go on safari in Africa.

A WEEK IN THE MOUNTAINS

Explore is a learning vacation in early fall for "active mature adults" over the age of 50. Set in Beaver Creek, in Vail Valley, Colorado, it offers symposia, hands-on workshops, and outdoor recreational clinics mixed with social activities. The symposia focus on a choice of topics from global political issues to art, history, geology, and astronomy. Workshops may include wildlife photography, literature, and mountain cooking, while the outdoor clinics range from fly fishing to golf dynamics.
For information: Explore, PO Box 2770, Avon, CO 81620; 800-323-4386.

EDUCATIONAL TRAVEL PROGRAMS

ALASKA SENIOR SEMINARS

The five-day off-season senior seminars offered by Alaska Wildland Adventures focus on Alaska's natural and cultural history, feature lectures, discussions, and field trips on topics such as bald eagles, the aurora borealis, glaciers, volcanoes and earthquakes, animal tracking, and native culture. They take place in spring or fall at Riverside Camp on the Kenai River, where you'll stay in a heated cabin or a cozy lodge and participate in indoor educational workshops interspersed with outdoor field trips.

For information: Alaska Wildland Adventures, PO Box 389, Girdwood, AK 99587; 800-334-8730.

ELDERFOLK

Each of Elderfolk's three- to five-week courses in Nepal, India, Tibet, Bhutan, China, and Pakistan focuses on Himalayan culture, history, natural history, religion, and arts and crafts. Several provide close looks at the native cuisines, and many include trekking. Exclusively for adventurers over the age of 55, they are offered by the Folkways Institute, which also plans study courses for students and professors.

Some of the courses, combining education and exotic travel, are cultural treks on which you'll be put up at night in roomy tents or lodges. Others are residential or overland trips where you lodge in small hotels or guest houses. Check out the Overland Journeys for Elderfolks—for example, the Ancient Silk Road trip, tracing Marco Polo's route from Beijing to Rawalpindi.

No previous knowledge or training is required, but some stamina definitely is.

For information: Folkways Institute, 14600 SE Aldridge Rd., Portland, OR 97236-6518; 800-225-4666 or 503-658-6600.

ELDERHOSTEL

Elderhostel, an educational travel program for older people who want to expand their horizons and learn a few more things, offers some of the world's best bargains. It is the clearinghouse for a network of over 1,900 colleges, universities, museums, national parks, conference centers, environmental education centers, and other cultural institutions that design and provide the faculty for low-cost residential learning programs for people 55 or older (and younger companions). Nearly a quarter-million people study with Elderhostel every year. The programs are offered in the United States and Canada as well as 48 countries overseas. Most Elderhostels in the U.S. and Canada last for five or six nights and start on a Sunday, while those in other countries are one to four weeks long and include stays at different institutions and sometimes different countries each week.

In most cases, you live in a campus dormitory, and take up to three courses chosen from a selection in the liberal arts and sciences taught by the host institution's faculty. There are no exams, grades, or homework. Nor do you get college credits for them. The courses and places to choose from are amazingly varied and many, an array of impressive proportions. The choices change every season and are rarely the same from year to year. Accommodations range from typical dorms to rustic cabins in the mountains to urban highrises at city universities. You will dine on campus food, simple but nourishing, and may use any of the school's recreational and cultural resources. Getting to and from the campus for the domestic programs is your responsibility.

Some of the domestic programs include active outdoor experiences such as camping, rafting, skiing, hiking, biking, or canoeing. If you are really into participation, you may even want to consider one of Elderhostel's Outward Bound or American Youth Hostel programs.

If you are interested in contributing your time and energy to a volunteer organization that provides significant services to meet real community needs all over the world, look into the Elderhostel Service Program. Elderhostel has recently joined forces with several national nonprofit organizations to create service opportunities for people over 55 (see Chapter 18).

If you want to take your adult children or grandchildren along, you'll find many intergenerational programs that are designed especially for you (see Chapter 3).

The international Elderhostel programs, one to four weeks long, usually combine morning classes with afternoon excursions, with the campus serving as home base as you study the culture, history, and lore of the land instructed by members of the university's faculty. Included in the overseas programs have been such far-out adventures as bike tours in England, France, and Holland (see Chapter 13).

There is sure to be a program in a place you've always wanted to visit, giving courses you've always wanted to take, at any time of the year. Check out the voluminous Elderhostel catalogs.

For information: Elderhostel, 75 Federal St., Boston, MA 02110; 617-426-7788. In Canada: Elderhostel Canada, 308 Wellington St., Kingston, ON K7K 7A7; 613-530-2222.

ELDERTREKS

The exotic adventures planned by ElderTreks to places such as China and Tibet, Thailand, and Borneo qualify as travel/study trips because they immerse you in the cultures you visit. See Chapter 5 for more.

For information: ElderTreks, 597 Markham St., Toronto, ON M6G 2L7; 800-741-7956 or 416-588-5000.

INTERHOSTEL

An international study/travel program for energetic people over the age of 50 (a companion need be only 40), Interhostel is sponsored by the University of New Hampshire. It offers two-week programs all over the world, from Africa to Europe, Australia, and South America. The idea is to stay in one country long enough to become well acquainted with the place you are visiting. During your stay, you will be introduced to the history, culture, and people through lectures, field trips, sightseeing excursions, and social and cultural activities. Your group, from 25 to 40 participants, will be accompanied by a representative of the university. Trips are scheduled year-round and are cosponsored by educational institutions in the host countries.

Living quarters, clean and comfortable although not necessarily fancy, are in residence halls or modest hotels. Most meals are cafeteria-style and feature the local food of the region. The cost, moderate for what you get, includes two weeks' full room and board, tuition, airfare, and ground transportation.

Because Interhostel's adventures impose a busy schedule of activities, you should be healthy and fit, full of vim and vigor, able to tote your own baggage, and walk comfortably at a moderate pace for at least a mile. **For information:** Interhostel, University of New Hampshire, 6 Garrison Ave., Durham, NH 03824; 800-733-9753.

NORTHEASTERN SENIOR SEMINARS

If you're 55 or older, you are eligible to enroll in a series of inexpensive one-week summer residential "campus vacations" at Skidmore College in upstate New York. You choose courses from a range of classes from economics to psychology to folk dancing, live in a dorm, and take part in activities on and off campus. If you like, you may enroll for two or three consecutive weeks with a different curriculum each week.

For information: Summer Special Programs, Skidmore College, Saratoga Springs, NY 12866-1632; 518-584-5000.

SAGA HOLIDAYS

Saga Holidays, marketing travel only for people over 50, offers travel/study programs as well as myriad escorted tours and cruises (see Chapter 5). One is its own series of Smithsonian Odyssey Tours, which take you to exotic parts of the world to learn from established conservation and wildlife experts. Another is its Road Scholar program, with itineraries that feature special educational themes, such as the mystery writers of England, some of whom serve as lecturers.

For information: Saga Holidays, 222 Berkeley St., Boston, MA 02116; 800-343-0273.

SENIOR VENTURES

A network of five colleges and universities in four western states—Oregon, Washington, Arizona, and California—offers people over 50 a chance to combine education with recreation and travel. College-level courses taught by faculty members offer everything from trout fishing to Shakespeare, interfaith studies, Native American culture, computer skills, the Oregon Trail, river rafting, southwestern ecology, and more. Most of the programs, which vary in length from one to four weeks, take place on college campuses and feature expeditions and field trips, but some take you on international adventures. Moderate fees cover virtually everything.

For information: Senior Ventures Network, Siskiyou Center, Southern Oregon State University, Ashland, OR 97520-5050; 800-257-0577.

UNIVERSITY VACATIONS (UNIVAC)

Open to students of all ages, including yours, Univac puts you up in a comfortable room for sessions of a week to 12 days in April, July, August, or September at Oxford or Cambridge in England, Trinity College in Ireland, Edinburgh University in Scotland, or the Sorbonne in Paris. Here mornings are spent attending a series of lectures presented by university scholars, with each session concentrating on a specific subject such as Chaucer's England, Medieval Life, Great Castles and Cathedrals, and American Writers in Paris. Afternoons are free for excursions or explorations. Again, the costs aren't likely to break the bank.

For information: Oxford-Cambridge Univac, 10461 NW 26th St., Miami, FL 33172; 800-792-0100 or 305-591-1736.

INSTITUTES FOR LEARNING IN RETIREMENT

Today there are more than 200 community-based Institutes for Learning in Retirement throughout the country that provide college-level courses on a noncredit basis for older adults. Each institute is sponsored by a college or university as a center for intellectual and social activity for its participants who are involved in determining curriculum, recruiting new members, and developing social programs.

In most cases, there are no tests or grades, although there may be assigned reading or other preparation. Students pay a modest annual membership fee and may usually take as many courses as they wish. At some institutions, they may take some regular undergraduate or adult education courses as well.

The following is a sampling of the learning programs. For a longer list and information about starting a new program, contact the Elderhostel Institute Network, an association of independent ILRs whose purpose is to extend the concept to new communities.

For information: Elderhostel Institute Network, 75 Federal St., Boston, MA 02110; 617-426-7788.

THE INSTITUTE FOR RETIRED PROFESSIONALS

This program, at the New School for Social Research in New York, was established in 1962, the first such program of its kind. As the granddaddy of them all, it has served as a pilot program for similar schools at other institutions. It offers its members—about 550 retired professionals—more than 70 study groups in subjects ranging from Great Decisions to Virginia Woolf to

Highlights of Mathematics to European history. Members may also enroll in one regular daytime New School course each semester.

For information: Institute for Retired Professionals, New School for Social Research, 66 W. 12th St., Room 502, New York, NY 10011; 212-229-5682.

ACADEMY OF LIFELONG LEARNING
For information: University of Delaware, 2800 Pennsylvania Ave., CED, Wilmington, DE 19806; 302-573-4433.

CENTER FOR CREATIVE RETIREMENT
For information: Long Island University, Southampton, NY 11968-4198; 516-283-4000.

CENTER FOR LEARNING IN RETIREMENT
For information: University of California Extension Center, 55 Laguna St., San Francisco, CA 94102; 415-863-4518.

DONOVAN SCHOLARS PROGRAM
A study program at the University of Kentucky in Lexington and at the 14 community colleges in Kentucky, the Donovan Scholars Program was designed specifically for students over the age of 65. It provides free tuition in all undergraduate or graduate courses in all academic areas. In addition, there are special noncredit course offerings for those over 60 in such subjects as art, music appreciation, radio drama, and exercise. Discussion groups meet twice a week and an annual week-long

writing workshop (for people over 57) is held every summer.

For information: Donovan Scholars Program, Ligon House, University of Kentucky, Lexington, KY 40506-0442; 606-257-2656.

NEVER TOO LATE TO LEARN

SeniorNet is an international nonprofit organization whose mission is to give older adults access to the information age by helping them learn computer skills and access SeniorNet Online, a telecommunications service. Headquartered in San Francisco, SeniorNet offers classes in common computer applications at its 63 Learning Centers throughout the country, on college campuses and in senior centers, hospitals, and retirement homes. As a member, you may use the equipment at the Centers or join the national online network using your own equipment. You can send electronic mail to other members; have access to electronic services, programs, and databases; participate in discussions; and take part in online conferences.

The $35 annual fee ($40 for couples) includes admission to Learning Centers, a free SeniorNet Online start-up kit, a quarterly newsletter, discounts on software, and special registration rates to conferences.

For information: SeniorNet, 399 Arguello Blvd., San Francisco, CA 94118; 415-750-5030.

DUKE INSTITUTE FOR LEARNING IN RETIREMENT

Here some of the classes are led by peers, while others are taught by university faculty and local professionals.

For information: Duke University, Durham, NC 27708; 919-684-6259.

THE HARVARD INSTITUTE FOR
LEARNING IN RETIREMENT
For information: Harvard Institute for Learning in Retirement, Lehman Hall B-3, Cambridge, MA 02138; 617-495-4973.

THE INSTITUTE FOR
LEARNING IN RETIREMENT
For information: The American University, Nebraska Hall, 4400 Massachusetts Ave. NW, Washington, DC 20016; 202-885-3920.

INSTITUTE OF NEW DIMENSIONS
This peer-learning school at three campuses of Palm Beach Community College offers retirees, for a small yearly fee, a choice of more than 160 courses a year plus individual lectures, special events, and an annual conference. Taught by volunteer faculty, the program is located on campuses in Lake Worth, Palm Beach Gardens, and West Palm Beach.
For information: Institute of New Dimensions, 4200 Congress Ave., Lake Worth, FL 33461; 407-439-8186.

NOVA COLLEGE INSTITUTE FOR
RETIRED PROFESSIONALS
For information: Nova College Institute for Retired Professionals, 3301 College Ave., Fort Lauderdale, FL 33314; 305-475-7036.

THE PLATO SOCIETY OF UCLA
For information: The Plato Society of UCLA, 10995 Le
Conte Ave., Los Angeles, CA 90024; 213-825-7917.

PROFESSIONALS AND EXECUTIVES
IN RETIREMENT
For information: Hofstra University, 1000 Hempstead
Turnpike, Hempstead, NY 11550; 516-560-6919.

TEMPLE ASSOCIATION FOR
RETIRED PROFESSIONALS
For information: Temple University, 1619 Walnut St.,
Philadelphia, PA 19103; 215-787-1505.

MORE GOOD WAYS
TO GET SMARTER

CHAUTAUQUA INSTITUTION

For 120 years, people have been traveling up to the
shores of Lake Chautauqua, in southwestern New York
State, to a cultural summer center set in a Victorian
village. The 856-acre hilltop complex offers a wide variety of educational programs, including summer weeks
and off-season weekends designed for people over the
age of 55. The 55-Plus Weekends and the Residential
Week for Older Adults are filled up far in advance, so if
you are interested, don't waste a moment before signing
up.

Each 55-Plus Weekend has a specific focus, such as
the U.S. Constitution, natural history, national politics,

music appreciation, or trade relations with Japan. They include discussions, workshops, lectures, films, recreational activities, and evening entertainment, all led by professionals. Housing and meals are available in a residence hall with double rooms and shared baths.

The Residential Weeks for Older Adults are similar but longer. And they include lodging and meals as well as admittance to other happenings at the center.

It's all quite cheap. The cost of tuition, room, meals, and planned activities for a Residential Week is currently only $375, while a 55-Plus Weekend costs $20 for commuters plus an additional $90 if you want accommodations and meals.

For information: Program Center for Older Adults, Chautauqua, NY 14722; 716-357-6200.

CLOSE UP FOUNDATION

An educational vacation in Washington, D.C., Close Up is designed for people who are at least 50. Its mission is to give you a week of firsthand access to "inside" Washington. Activities include two or three seminars a day with key Washington personalities (senators, White House officials, foreign ambassadors, reporters, and others) on topics of current concern; daily briefings for background information; motorcoach tours of the city; a day on Capitol Hill; all meals, many at restaurants; an evening at the theater; daily workshops to discuss issues and events; a banquet; and scheduled free time. You'll lodge in a good hotel.

All this, available to both groups and individuals, is quite inexpensive. That's because the weeks are offered in the spring and fall by the Close Up Foundation, a nonprofit, nonpartisan organization that has brought more than 375,000 people of all ages to Washington to study government on location, in cooperation with the American Association of Retired Persons (AARP).

The Close Up Foundation also runs a Congressional Senior Citizen Intern Program, where you spend a week working in the office of your own member of Congress (contact your senator or representative to be considered for this program). The qualifications: you must be 60, healthy, and willing to work.
For information: Close Up Foundation, 44 Canal Center Plaza, Alexandria, VA 22314; 800-232-2000 or 703-706-3668.

THE COLLEGE AT 60
Part of Fordham University and located at the Lincoln Center campus in New York City, the College at 60 offers credit courses in liberal arts subjects such as history, psychology, philosophy, economics, literature, music, art, and computers, taught by Fordham faculty members. Included are a lecture series and the use of all college facilities. After taking four seminars, students receive a certificate and are encouraged to enter the regular Fordham University program.

Believe it or not, you are eligible for the College at 60 when you are 50.
For information: The College at 60, Fordham University at Lincoln Center, 113 W. 60th St., Room 422, New York, NY 10023; 212-636-6740.

CORNELL'S ADULT UNIVERSITY
In July of every year, Cornell's Adult University sponsors week-long seminars at its campus at Ithaca, NY,

where you may take courses in a wide variety of subjects in liberal arts, science, and business. Currently, the program costs around $700, including room and board. In addition, study tours are offered off-campus at sites around the country and abroad, in such places as Dublin, London, Wyoming, and Martha's Vineyard.

For information: Cornell's Adult University, 626 Thurston Ave., Ithaca, NY 14850-2490; 607-255-6260.

NORTH CAROLINA CENTER FOR CREATIVE RETIREMENT

The NCCR involves more than 1,500 50-plus participants every year in its five-component program: the College for Seniors, in which members teach and learn together; a leadership for seniors program, which explores the history, civic life, and challenges of the community; two intergenerational mentoring programs—one matching retirees with university undergraduates, the other placing senior volunteers in area public schools; and a retirement relocation weekend program that covers everything from housing options to hiking trails in western North Carolina.

For information: The North Carolina Center for Creative Retirement, University of North Carolina at Asheville, Asheville, NC 28804-3299; 704-251-6140.

OASIS

OASIS (Older Adult Service and Information System) is a nonprofit organization sponsored by the May Department Stores Company in collaboration with local hospitals, medical centers, government agencies, and other participants in 30 locations across the nation. Its pur-

pose is to enrich the lives of people over 55 by providing educational, cultural, and wellness programs to its members. At its centers, OASIS offers classes ranging from French conversation and the visual arts to dance, bridge, creative writing, history, exercise, classical music, points of law, and prevention of osteoporosis. Also featured are special events such as concerts, plays, and museum exhibits; lectures; volunteer opportunities; and even trips and cruises. If you live in an OASIS city, sign up—this is a good deal. Membership is free.
For information: The OASIS Institute, 7710 Carondelet Ave., Ste. 125, St. Louis, MO 63105; 314-862-2933.

UNIVERSITY SENIORS
Membership in this New York University program for people over 65 gets you two university courses in the School of Continuing Education per semester plus biweekly luncheon seminars on subjects of current interest, all for a moderate fee. Recent topics have included Coping with Crime, Truth in the Media, and Glories of the Opera.
For information: University Seniors, NYU School of Continuing Education, 11 W. 42nd St., New York, NY 10036; 212-790-1330.

GETTING AN EDUCATION IN CANADA
Virtually every college and university in Canada offers free tuition to students over the age of 60 or 65, whether they attend classes part-time or full-time. Col-

leges of applied arts and technology generally offer postsecondary credit courses through their Departments of Continuing Education or Extension to seniors and charge only a few dollars per course. Aside from the nonexistent or low cost, seniors are treated just like the other students, have the same privileges, and must abide by the same regulations.

For information: Write to the registrar of the college you've chosen for information about its program or, for general information, to the Ministry of Colleges and Universities in your province.

NATIONAL ACADEMY OF OLDER CANADIANS

Based in Vancouver, the NAOC's mission is to involve older Canadians in lifelong learning and to work in partnership with other nonprofit organizations to develop programs to promote its membership's contribution to society. These programs currently include computer classes, business training, workshops, learning circles, mentoring, town meetings, and discussion groups on issues of special interest. Annual membership fee is $15.

For information: National Academy of Older Canadians, 411 Dunsmuir St., Vancouver, BC V6B 1X4.

Chapter Seventeen

Shopping Breaks, Taxes, Insurance, and Other Practical Matters

T his chapter is not filled with great suggestions for having fun, but the information here may tip you off to some facts you didn't know as well as benefits that are coming your way simply because you've lived so long.

SAVING MONEY IN THE STORES

Clever marketing experts have recently realized that the over-50s, a segment now growing three times faster than the rest of the country's population, is the next target market. We not only have more money to spend but are more inclined to spend it than younger consumers. On the other hand, we're a bunch of cautious consumers who know the value of a dollar and are always on the lookout for a bargain.

MONTGOMERY WARD

Montgomery Ward's Y.E.S. (Years of Extra Savings) Discount Club, a very good deal indeed, saves you money in many ways when you've reached the magic age of 55. As a member, you receive a membership card and a bimonthly magazine. The membership fee is currently

$2.99 per month for you and your spouse. With the membership card in hand, you will get 10 percent off any merchandise, sale or nonsale, in Montgomery Ward stores every Tuesday. On Tuesdays, Wednesdays, and Thursdays, you're entitled to 10 percent off any auto labor charges.

What's more, the Y.E.S. Club Travel Service plans your travel, makes reservations, and gives you good discounted prices plus cash rebates on the cost of your trips. This means that upon your return you will receive a check for a 10 percent rebate on all lodging and car rentals, and 5 percent on tours, cruises, rail passes, and airline tickets.

For information: Montgomery Ward Y.E.S. Discount Club, 200 N. Martingale Rd., Schaumburg, IL 60173; 800-421-5396.

FEDERAL INCOME TAXES

The tax laws no longer provide an extra exemption for people over the age of 65. Instead, they give you a larger standard deduction than younger people are entitled to, according to Julian Block, tax attorney and author of a guide to saving money on income taxes, *It's Not What You Make—It's What You Keep.*

The standard deductions for everyone *under* 65 for 1995 returns are $6,550 for married couples filing jointly; $3,275 each for married people filing separately; $3,900 for single people, and $5,750 for heads of households. These standard deductions change every year to reflect inflation, so be sure to check them out for each year's return.

If one spouse of a couple filing jointly is *over* 65, the standard deduction is increased for 1995 returns (by $750) to $7,300. If both members of a married couple are over 65, it is increased (by $750 twice) to $8,050.

For a married person over 65 filing separately, the deduction increases (by $750) to $4,025. A single person over 65 may deduct $4,850 ($950 more than those who are younger). And a head of household over 65 gets a standard deduction in 1995 of $6,700 ($950 more than an under-65).

None of this applies, of course, if you itemize your deductions.

By the way, the Internal Revenue Service issues a free booklet, *Tax Information for Older Americans* (Publication No. 554), which you can get at your local IRS office or by calling 800-TAX-FORM. You may also want to ask for its free *Guide to Free Tax Services* (Publication No. 910), which provides a list of IRS booklets on federal taxes and explains what each one covers.

SALE OF PRINCIPAL RESIDENCE

You can save money on taxes if you or your spouse is 55 when you sell the home you have owned and lived in as a principal residence for at least three years out of the five-year period ending on the date of the sale. You may elect to exclude from your income for federal tax purposes up to $125,000 if you are single or married and filing a joint return. You may exclude $62,500 each if you are married and filing separately.

As much as $250,000 can be tax-free on the sale of a residence owned jointly by individuals who are not husband and wife—for example, a parent and child, a brother and sister, or an unmarried couple sharing quarters. As long as each unmarried joint owner is over 55, each gets to exclude up to $125,000 of his or her share of the profit. But when one is under 55 and the other over 55, only the older owner is eligible for the tax break.

Before you decide to take advantage of this, however, be sure to discuss it with a tax consultant because this exclusion may be used only once in your lifetime and you may be better off saving the privilege for a later home sale.

HOW TO GET HELP WITH YOUR TAX RETURN

Assistance in preparing your tax returns is available free from both the Internal Revenue Service and AARP. The IRS offers Tax Counseling for the Elderly (TCE) for people over 60 (and Voluntary Income Tax Assistants for younger people who need help). Trained volunteers provide information and will prepare returns at thousands of sites throughout the country from February 2 to April 15. Watch your local newspaper for a list of sites in your area or call 800-TAX-1040 and press 0.

Or you may contact the Tax-Aide service provided by the American Association of Retired Persons (see Chapter 19), which is one of the sponsors of TCE. At its sites, tax counselors help low- and moderate-income taxpayers over 60 to complete their forms. The sites will be listed in the newspapers along with those of the IRS. Or you may call your local IRS office for the location nearest you.

AUTO AND HOMEOWNER'S INSURANCE

Mature people tend to be good drivers, becoming a much better risk class as a group than the younger crowd. They tend to be more careful drivers, having shed most of their bad habits, and drive fewer miles. Therefore, statistically, they have about 10 percent fewer accidents per year than other risk categories do. These are the reasons many insurance companies offer discounts on automobile coverage once you've reached a certain age.

Some companies even offer reductions in premiums for homeowner's insurance as well, figuring you have become a more cautious and reliable sort who takes good care of your property.

Although discounts are wonderful and we all love to get them, they are not the whole picture, according to The National Insurance Consumers Organization, which advises that you "shop the bottom line" rather than discounts alone, always considering what you pay for the coverage you get. If a company charges higher premiums than other companies for comparable coverage and then gives you a discount, you haven't profited at all.

Because insurance regulations differ from state to state, a complete list of companies giving discounts for age is impossible to assemble. It is best to go through an insurance company or agent or your state's insurance department. The following, however, are some of the special offerings of major firms in many states.

AETNA

In most states, Aetna gives a 15 percent discount on liability, comprehensive, and collision coverage to good drivers ages 55 to 64 who use their cars only for pleasure driving. Good drivers 65 to 74 get 25 percent off across the board, while those over the age of 75 are entitled to 10 percent if they satisfy certain health criteria. At all ages, if state regulations allow, you get an additional discount if both your auto and homeowners insurance are with Aetna.

HOW TO SAVE YOUR LIFE

If you happen to get sick or have an accident while you're away from home, a nonprofit foundation called **Medic-Alert** may save your health or even your life. When you join, at an annual fee of $15, you will receive a metal bracelet or neck chain engraved with your personal identification number and a 24-hour-a-day call-collect telephone number tied into a national data bank. When you or medical personnel call the data bank, all of your backup medical information is provided along with names and telephone numbers of your physician, next of kin, people to notify in an emergency, and other relevant information. As a backup, you get a wallet card with the same information. If you have an implanted medical device such as a pacemaker, heart valve, or breast implant, you may ask to be listed in MedicAlert's Implant Registry Service, which will alert you to recalls and safety information about your device.

For information: MedicAlert Foundation, PO Box 1009, Turlock, CA 95381; 800-ID-ALERT (800-432-5378).

ALLSTATE

Allstate gives a 10 percent discount across the board—for all coverage—on both auto and homeowner's policies to people who are at least 55 and retired.

KEEP AN INVENTORY OF
HOUSEHOLD GOODS

A free booklet, *Nonbusiness Disaster, Casualty and Theft Loss Workbook* (Publication No. 584), available from the Internal Revenue Service, is designed to help you determine the amount of a casualty or theft loss deduction for household goods and personal property. You use the booklet to list your possessions on a room-by-room basis, with space to record the number of items, date acquired, cost, value, and amount of loss. It is not easy to make a complete inventory of your possessions, but it is easier than trying to remember all those details after a theft or fire. Pick the booklet up at your local IRS office or call 800-TAX-FORM.

CHUBB

Chubb's offer is a 7 to 10 percent reduction of the premium on liability, collision, and comprehensive automobile coverage for drivers over 50. Cars must be used for pleasure only, and there may be no drivers under the age of 25 in the household.

COLONIAL PENN

This company gives a retirement discount if you use your car only for pleasure.

GEICO

In most states, Geico gives good drivers between the ages of 50 and 75, retired or not, a lower rate on all automobile coverages on the cars they principally operate and are not used for business. A certificate from an accredited defensive-driving course may give you an additional 10 percent discount. Over-50s are also eligible for a multirisk plan that gives them "mechanical breakdown" coverage on new cars in addition to comprehensive and collision coverages. And that's not all. A Prime Time contract, available in some states, gives you the same coverage, again at lower rates, and adds a guaranteed renewal provision stating that your policy may not be canceled for reasons of age, accidents, or driving violations. To get this contract, the principal operator of the household must be over 50, no one on the policy may be under 25, and your record must be free of accidents and violations for at least three years.

As for homeowners coverage, Geico offers a 20 percent reduction in the premium for those over 50 and retired, except in Arizona, where you get 25 percent; in Pennsylvania and New York, where the discount is 10 percent; and in Texas, where it is 5 percent.

ITT HARTFORD

The company that services the American Association of Retired Persons (see Chapter 19) offers members of this organization a discount of about 10 percent for completing an accredited defensive-driving course and up to 10 percent for maintaining a safe driving record. There are also lifetime renewal agreements, credits for low annual mileage, and full 12-month policies.

On homeowner's insurance, ITT Hartford offers 5 percent credit on your total premium at any age in most states if you are retired.

LIBERTY MUTUAL

Special discounted rates are given by Liberty Mutual across the board on automobile insurance starting at age 50 and increasing at 65.

NATIONWIDE

In some states, Nationwide gives a discount of 10 percent on all automobile coverage for people 55 and over.

PRUDENTIAL

In many states, you'll get a mature homeowner's discount of 5 percent from Prudential when you've reached 55. And, if you take a "55 Alive" defensive-driving course, you will be entitled to up to 10 percent off on your automobile insurance.

BANKING

Many banks offer special incentives and services to people over 55 or 60, ranging from free checking to free NOW accounts, elimination of savings-account fees, free insurance, travelers cheques, and safe-deposit boxes, and even cash rebates at restaurants. Every bank and every state is different, so you must check out the situation in your community. Do some careful comparison shopping to make sure you are getting the best deal available.

LEGAL ASSISTANCE

Call upon your local area senior agency, which is required by law to provide some legal assistance to older citizens. Yours may help you untangle some puzzling legal problems or, at least, tell you what services are available to you. Or contact the local bar association for information. It is quite possible that it operates a referral or pro bono program. Or, suggests the American Bar Association, ask your local Legal Services Program for help or referrals.

HOW TO FIND LOCAL ELDER SERVICES

For information about housing, home health, legal assistance, or other kinds of services for older people, call the Eldercare Locator at 800-677-1116. This nationwide governmental resource for elderly people or their caregivers will help you find an appropriate agency or program in your area. Call between 9 A.M. and 8 P.M. (Eastern Time) Monday through Friday and explain the problem. Be sure you know the zip code of the person needing help.

Chapter Eighteen
Volunteer for
Great Experiences

There's no need to let your talents and energy go to waste once you have stopped working for a living. If, perhaps for the first time in your life, you have hours to spare, maybe you'd like to spend some of them volunteering your services to organizations that could use your help. There is plenty of work waiting for you. If you are looking for a good match between your abilities and a program that needs them, consider the programs detailed here, all of them eager to take advantage of your years of experience.

But, first, keep in mind:

Remember, when you file your federal income tax, you are allowed to deduct unreimbursed expenses incurred while volunteering your services. These include transportation, parking, tolls, meals and lodging (in some cases), and uniforms.

RSVP (RETIRED AND SENIOR VOLUNTEER PROGRAM)

RSVP, an organization that receives funding, support, and technical assistance from the Corporation for National Service, the federal domestic volunteer agency, and functions under the auspices of local service organizations, matches the interests and abilities of men and women over 55 with part-time volunteer opportunities in their own communities. As an RSVP volunteer, you may be assigned to work in schools, libraries, courts, day-care centers, crisis centers, hospitals, nursing homes, or economic development agencies. You may get involved in tax aid, home repair, counseling, refugee assistance, home visitation, adult education, or whatever other services are needed in your area. You will serve without pay but may be reimbursed for or provided with transportation and other expenses. You may work for only several hours a week or many more than that if you wish.

For information: Contact your local or regional RSVP office or Corporation for National Service, 1100 Vermont Ave. NW, Washington, DC 20525; 800-424-8867 or 202-606-5000.

THE SERVICE CORPS OF RETIRED EXECUTIVES

SCORE is a national organization of both active and retired professionals and business executives who offer their expertise free of charge to small businesses. SCORE counselors, who include lawyers, business executives, accountants, engineers, managers, journalists, and other specialists, provide management assistance and advice to small-business people who are going into business or who are already in business but need expert help.

With a current membership of more than 12,000 men and women, SCORE has about 400 chapters all over the

mainland United States as well as Puerto Rico, Guam, and the Virgin Islands. Funded and coordinated by the government's Small Business Administration, it is operated and administered by its own elected officials.
For information: Contact your local U.S. Small Business Administration office or SCORE, 409 Third St. SW, Ste. 5900, Washington, DC 20416; 800-634-0245 or 202-205-6762.

JOB PROGRAM FOR OLDER WORKERS

Senior Community Service Employment Program (SCSEP), a federally funded program, recruits unemployed low-income men and women over the age of 55, assesses their employment strengths, and hires them for paid jobs in community-service positions. At the same time, the enrollees begin training in new job skills, receive such help as counseling, physical examinations, group meetings, and job fairs while the agency tries to match them with permanent jobs in the private sector. If you qualify and are looking for a paying position, this agency is worth a try.
For information: SCSEP, National Council on the Aging, 409 Third St. SW, Washington, DC 20024; 202-479-1200. Or contact your local, county, or state Office for the Aging.

AARP VOLUNTEER TALENT BANK

This useful service was organized by AARP, the vast over-50 club (see Chapter 19), to help those who wish to serve others. Says a spokesperson, "People over 50 have a lifetime of experience and skills which can apply to a variety of volunteer interests," and the Talent Bank puts people and work together. After you complete a questionnaire about your background, special interests, and skills, the information is matched by computer with opportunities for volunteer work within the American Association of Retired Persons or by referral to other organizations in your own community.

For information: AARP Volunteer Talent Bank, 601 E St. NW, Washington, DC 20049; 202-434-AARP.

PEACE CORPS

No doubt you've always thought the Peace Corps was reserved for young idealists right out of college. The truth is that it's a viable choice for idealists of any age. Eighty is the upper age limit for acceptance into the Peace Corps, and since its beginning in 1961 thousands of Senior Volunteers have brought their talents and experience to developing countries in Latin America, the Caribbean, Africa, Asia, and the Pacific. To become a Senior Volunteer, you must be a U.S. citizen and meet basic legal and medical criteria. Some assignments require a college or technical-school degree or an experience equivalent. Married couples are eligible and will be assigned together.

What you get in return is the chance to travel, an unforgettable living experience in a foreign land, basic expenses, and housing, plus technical, language, and cultural training. And you will have a chance to use your expertise constructively in fields such as agriculture, engineering, math/science, home economics, education, skilled trades, forestry and fisheries, and community development.

For information: Peace Corps, 1990 K St. NW, Washington, DC 20526; 800-424-8580.

SENIOR ENVIRONMENTAL EMPLOYMENT PROGRAM (SEE)

The SEE Program, administered by the Environmental Protection Agency (EPA), establishes grants to private nonprofit organizations to recruit, hire, and pay people over the age of 55 to help fight environmental pollution. The recruits, who work part-time or full-time in EPA offices or in the field, are paid by the hour in jobs that assist the agency in protecting the environment and cleaning up America.

For information: Contact your regional EPA office or SEE Program, EPA, 401 M St. SW, Washington, DC 20460; 202-260-2574.

VOLUNTEERS IN TECHNICAL ASSISTANCE

VITA provides another avenue for helping developing countries. A nonprofit international organization, VITA provides volunteer experts who respond—usually by direct correspondence—to technical inquiries from people in these nations who need assistance in such areas as small-business development, energy applications, agriculture, reforestation, water supply and sanitation, and low-cost housing. Its volunteers also perform other services such as project planning, translations, publications, marketing strategies, evaluations, and technical reports and often become on-site consultants.

There is no minimum age, but you must be retired to serve. If you become a volunteer, you will not be paid, but you will be reimbursed for your travel and living expenses.

For information: Volunteers in Technical Assistance, 1600 Wilson Blvd., Ste. 500, Arlington, VA 22209; 703-276-1800.

SENIOR COMPANIONS

Senior Companions are income-eligible Americans 60 or over who volunteer four hours a day, five days a week, to provide services and companionship for the homebound, helping them maintain their independence. In a program funded and supported by the Corporation for National Service and by local agencies, the volunteers help other people cope with life. For example, they assist disabled veterans, recovering mental patients, Alzheimer's patients, the blind, recovering substance abusers, men and women recuperating from major surgery or illnesses, and those who are in chronic frail health.

Although the volunteers are not paid, they receive a modest nontaxable stipend that does not affect social security eligibility, reimbursement for transportation and meals, on-duty insurance, and an annual physical exam.

For information: Corporation for National Service, 1100 Vermont Ave. NW, Washington, DC 20525; 800-424-8867 or 202-606-5000.

VOLUNTEER GRANDPARENTS SOCIETY

The objective of this nonprofit organization in Canada is to match volunteer grandparents with families with children between the ages of 3 and 12 who have no accessible grandparents. The job of the volunteers, who are not paid and do not commit to a contract or specific hours, is to establish a relationship of mutual enjoyment, support, and caring and to become part of an extended family. Applicants are interviewed and carefully screened, and matches are based on compatibility as well as on geographic proximity. The organization,

which originated in 1973 in Vancouver, has expanded into other areas in the province of British Columbia and serves as a model for similar agencies in Ottawa and Toronto.
For information: Volunteer Grandparents, #3, 1734 W. Broadway, Vancouver, BC V6J 1Y1.

FOSTER GRANDPARENTS PROGRAM

This federal program sponsored by the government's national volunteer agency offers gratifying volunteer work to thousands of income-eligible men and women 60 and over, in communities all over the 50 states, Puerto Rico, Virgin Islands, and the District of Columbia. The volunteers, who receive 40 hours of preservice orientation and training and four hours a month of in-service training, work with children who have special needs— boarder babies; troubled children; handicapped, severely retarded, abandoned, delinquent, abused, hospitalized, addicted, forlorn children who are desperate for love, care, and attention and do not get it from their families. They may work in hospitals, schools, homes, day-care programs, or residential centers.

Volunteers, who must be in good health although they may be handicapped, work 20 hours a week. For this, they receive, aside from the immense satisfaction, a small tax-free annual stipend, a transportation allowance, hot meals while at work, accident and liability insurance, and annual physicals.
For information: Contact your local Foster Grandparents program, or the Corporation for National Service, 1100 Vermont Ave. NW, Washington, DC 20525; 800-424-8867 or 202-606-5000.

FAMILY FRIENDS

A national program sponsored by the National Council on Aging, Family Friends recruits volunteers over the age of 55 to work with children with disabilities, chronic illnesses, or other problems in 30 locations around the country. The volunteers act as caring grandparents, helping the families in whatever ways they can, mostly dealing with children at home but occasionally in hospitals. They are asked to serve at least four hours a week and to commit themselves to the program for at least a year.

The local projects are funded by the federal government, corporations, foundations, and local, county, city, or state governments.

For information: Family Friends Resource Center, 409 Third St. SW, Washington, DC 20024; 202-479-6675.

INTERNATIONAL EXECUTIVE SERVICE CORPS

IESC, organized and directed by U.S. business executives, is a nonprofit organization that recruits retired, highly skilled executives and technical advisors to assist businesses in the developing nations. It is funded by the U.S. Agency for International Development (AID), overseas clients and foreign governments, and many American corporations.

After being briefed on the country and the client, volunteer executives travel overseas—with their spouses, if they wish—for projects that generally last two to three months. IESC pays for the couple's travel expenses and provides a per diem allowance.

For information: International Executive Service Corps, 333 Ludlow St., Stamford, CT 06902; 800-243-4372 or 203-967-6000.

FOR JOB HUNTERS

If you're over 40 and in the market for a job but don't know where to start looking for one, hook up with Operation ABLE, a nonprofit organization affiliated with agencies that will help match you with a likely employer. You're in luck if you live in Chicago, where there are five regional offices. In addition, there is a network of independent ABLE-like organizations, modeled after the original, in several other cities, including New York, Boston, Denver, Los Angeles, Atlanta, Seattle, and Little Rock.

Operation ABLE tries every which way to get you into the working world. It provides job counseling, on-the-job training, group training activities, and individual career assessment and guidance; teaches job-hunting skills; matches older workers with employers; operates a pool of temporaries; and offers myriad other services. **For information:** Operation ABLE, 180 N. Wabash Ave., Chicago, IL 60601; 312-782-3335.

SHEPHERD'S CENTERS OF AMERICA (SCA)

An interfaith, nonprofit organization of older adults who volunteer their skills to help seniors in their communities, SCA has 95 centers in 26 states and one in Canada. Supported by Catholic, Jewish, and Protestant congregations as well as businesses and foundations, the centers operate many programs designed to enable older people to remain in their own homes as active participants in community life. Centers offer such in-home services as Telephone Visitors, Family Friends, Meals on Wheels, Handyhands Service, and Respite Care, all provided mostly by volunteers. Programs at the centers include other services, day trips, classes and courses as well as support groups and referrals. Membership is open to anyone over the age of 55.

For information: Shepherd's Centers of America, 6700 Troost Ave., Suite 616, Kansas City, MO 64131; 800-547-7073 or 816-523-1080.

NATIONAL EXECUTIVE SERVICE CORPS

This nonprofit organization performs a unique service: it helps other nonprofit organizations solve their problems by providing retired executives with extensive corporate and professional experience to serve as volunteer consultants. Its services are offered in five basic areas—education, health, the arts, social services, and religion—and the assistance covers everything from organizational structure and financial systems to marketing and funding strategy. Volunteers' expenses are covered.

For information: National Executive Service Corps, 257 Park Ave. South, New York, NY 10010; 212-529-6660.

NATIONAL PARK SERVICE

If you love the outdoors and have the time, volunteer to work for the National Park Service as a VIP (Volunteers in Parks). VIPs are not limited to over-50s, but a good portion of them are retired people with time, expertise, talent, and interest in forests and wilderness. You may work a few hours a week or a month, seasonally or full-time, and may or may not—depending on the park—wear a uniform or get reimbursed for out-of-pocket expenses. The job possibilities range from working at an information desk to serving as a guide, maintaining trails, driving a shuttle bus, painting fences, designing computer programs, patrolling trails, making wildlife counts, writing visitor brochures, and preparing park events.

For information: Contact the VIP coordinator at the national park where you would like to volunteer and request an application. Or, for addresses, contact the appropriate National Park Service regional office.

ELDERHOSTEL/HABITAT FOR HUMANITY

Sign up via Elderhostel to become a volunteer for Habitat for Humanity International, an ecumenical, non-profit, Christian organization with a goal of eliminating substandard housing. You will help build new homes and rehabilitate existing ones, in partnership with home-owners. Elderhostelers may currently choose to work in one of five disadvantaged communities in the U.S.

For information: Elderhostel Service Programs, 75 Federal St., Boston, MA 02110-1941; 617-426-7788.

ELDERHOSTEL/GLOBAL VOLUNTEERS

The goal of nonprofit, nonsectarian Global Volunteers is "to help establish a foundation for world peace through mutual understanding based on citizen-to-citizen contact." It sends volunteers to work for up to four weeks in rural communities in a variety of developing and Eastern European countries as the guest of a host organization. Sign up via Elderhostel to join other over-55 volunteers in Jamaica (where you may teach, provide health care, work on construction projects), Poland (where your job will be to teach English in rural areas outside of

Warsaw), or Indonesia (where you'll teach English and maintain school buildings).

For information: Elderhostel Service Programs, 75 Federal St., Boston, MA 02110-1941; 617-426-7788.

ELDERHOSTEL/OCEANIC SOCIETY EXPEDITIONS

Oceanic Society Expeditions is a nonprofit group that organizes ecology-related field research expeditions to many places around the world, providing a way for people to become involved in the scientific study of global environmental issues. In this case, through the auspices of Elderhostel, volunteers over the age of 55 help researchers make observations, gather and analyze data, and perform other useful tasks. Current project sites include the Amazon River in Peru, where you will collect information on the ecology of the endangered pink river dolphin, and Belize, where you will assist scientists in recording bird calls and songs, studying bottlenose dolphins, or observing the behavior of black howler monkeys.

For information: Elderhostel Service Programs, 75 Federal St., Boston, MA 02110-1941; 617-426-7788.

ELDERHOSTEL/DOUBLE H HOLE IN THE WOODS

A recent addition to Elderhostel's volunteer service programs is the Double H Hole in the Woods Ranch, for critically ill and severely handicapped children between six and 16. Founded by actor Paul Newman, the ranch gives the over-55 volunteers jobs such as working in the infirmary, helping with the animals, teaching swimming, mentoring, or just being surrogate grandparents. **For information:** Elderhostel Service Programs, 75 Federal St., Boston MA 02110-1941; 617-426-7788.

FORTY PLUS CLUBS

Offices in 21 cities throughout the United States comprise this nonprofit cooperative of unemployed executives, managers, and professionals, men and women, 40 years of age or more. Their objective is to help members conduct effective job searches and find new jobs. There is no paid staff. The members do all the work and help pay expenses with their one-time charge of from $300 to $600, depending on location (paid in installments), plus moderate dues. They must commit themselves to attend weekly meetings and spend at least two days a week working at the club and assisting others in their search for work.

In return, members are helped to examine their career skills and define their goals, counseled on résumé writing and interview skills, helped to plan marketing strategy, and given job leads. They may also use the club as a base of operations, with phone answering and mail service, computers, and reference library.

Forty Plus Clubs exist at this writing in New York City and Buffalo, New York; Oakland, San Diego, San Jose, and Los Angeles (with a branch in Laguna Hills), California; Lakewood, Colorado; Chicago, Illinois; Columbus, Ohio; Dallas and Houston, Texas; Murray, Ogden, and Provo, Utah; Philadelphia, Pennsylvania; Bellevue, Washington; Washington, D.C.; St. Paul, Minnesota, and Honolulu, Hawaii.

For information: Addresses of the clubs and descriptive material are available from Forty Plus of New York, 15 Park Row, New York, NY 10038; 212-233-6086.

VOLUNTEER PROGRAMS IN ISRAEL

ACTIVE RETIREES IN ISRAEL (ARI)

Sponsored by B'nai B'rith International, ARI is a volunteer work program for people who are 50, in good health, and members of B'nai B'rith. Volunteers pay for the opportunity to live in the resort city of Netanya and work in the mornings for two-and-a-half winter months in hospitals, forests, kibbutzim, schools, and facilities for the elderly and the handicapped. Afternoons are spent learning Hebrew, while the evenings include concerts, discussion groups, and cultural activities. Guided tours of the country are part of the program.

For information: ARI, B'nai B'rith Israel Commission, 1640 Rhode Island Ave. NW, Washington, DC 20036; 800-500-6533 or 202-857-6580.

WINTER AND SPRING IN NETANYA PROGRAMS

Hadassah's Winter in Netanya (WIN) and Springtime in Netanya (SPIN) programs send volunteers to Israel for one or two months to work, study, and absorb Israeli culture. For a month in December, for two months in January and February, or for a month in the spring, American participants live in a four-star hotel in Netanya, a Mediterranean resort town 20 miles north of Tel Aviv. Here the volunteer workers, most of them retirees, spend their mornings working at the local hospital, tutoring schoolchildren in English, packing supplies for the Israel Defense Forces, pruning and planting trees, visiting senior centers, painting murals, or doing carpentry. Afternoons are devoted to conversational Hebrew lessons and sightseeing tours, while evenings are reserved for social and cultural events.

For information: Hadassah, 50 West 58th St., New York, NY 10019; 212-303-8133 or your local Hadassah chapter.

JNF CANADIAN AND AMERICAN ACTIVE RETIREES IN ISRAEL (CAARI)

To qualify for this two-month program sponsored by the Jewish National Fund, you must be over 50 and in good enough shape to work. Your first month will be spent working five mornings a week, tending the JNF national forests and, in addition, working at a choice of other jobs. Some volunteers choose to contribute their time in schools, hospitals, homes for the aged, army bases, universities, or kibbutzim, while others assist local craftspeople or archaeologists. Afternoons are devoted to planned activities, including Hebrew lessons, and evenings are devoted to socializing. For your second month, you'll tour the country and spend time in Jerusalem.

For information: JNF CAARI Program, Missions Dept., 42 E. 69th St., New York, NY 10021; 800-223-7787 or 212-879-9300, extension 283.

VOLUNTEERS FOR ISRAEL

In this volunteer work-and-cultural program for adults 18 and older in Israel, you'll put in eight-hour days for three weeks, sleep in a segregated dormitory, and work in small groups at a reserve or supply military base, doing whatever needs doing most at that moment. You may serve in supply, warehousing, or maintenance of equipment or in social services in hospitals. You'll wear an army uniform with a "Civilian Volunteer" patch. Board, room, and other expenses are free, but you must pay for your own partially subsidized airfare.

For information: Volunteers for Israel, 330 West 42nd St., 18th floor, New York, NY 10036-6902; 212-643-4848.

AARP WORKS

A series of eight job-search workshops on employment planning, AARP Works is now offered twice a year at about 80 locations in 30 states. Led by AARP volunteer teams and community agencies, the workshops help midlife and older job seekers to identify and redefine their skills, interests, and work experience; explore ways to overcome obstacles to employment, such as age discrimination; and learn effective job-search techniques. A nominal fee is charged for materials.

For information: For locations, dates, and cost, contact your nearest AARP area office or AARP Works, Work Force Programs Dept., 601 E St. NW, Washington, DC 20049.

Chapter Nineteen

The Over-50 Organizations and What They Can Do for You

W hen you consider that there are more people in this country over the age of 55 than there are children in elementary and high schools, you can see why we have powerful potential to influence what goes on around here. As the demographic discovery of the decade, a group that controls most of the nation's disposable income, we've become an enormous marketing target. And, just like any other group of people, we've got plenty of needs.

A number of organizations in the United States and Canada have been formed in the last few years to act as advocates for the over-50 crowd and to offer us special deals and services. Here is a brief rundown on them and what they have to offer you. You may want to join more than one of them so you can reap the benefits of each.

THE AMERICAN ASSOCIATION OF RETIRED PERSONS

AARP is a nonprofit community-service organization, the biggest, oldest, and best known of all such organizations, with a vast array of services and programs. With about 33 million members, AARP is open to anyone anywhere in the world who's over 50, retired or not, and so it wields amazing power in the marketplace and among the nation's policy makers. Its bimonthly magazine, *Modern Maturity*, and its monthly *Bulletin* go to more people than any other publications in the country.

For a yearly membership fee of $8 (and that includes a spouse), AARP offers so many things that you are likely to stop reading before you get to the end of the list. But here are some of them:

▶ Supplemental health insurance at group rates.
▶ A nonprofit, mail-order pharmacy service that delivers by mail.
▶ Discounts on hotels, motels, resorts, and auto rentals.
▶ A travel service that offers preplanned tours and discounted cruises especially for mature voyagers.
▶ A motor club that gets you emergency road and towing service, trip planning, and other benefits.
▶ Auto and homeowner's insurance tailored for people over 50.
▶ A bimonthly magazine, full of general articles and useful information, plus a monthly news bulletin.
▶ A national advocacy and lobbying program to develop legislative objectives and priorities and represent the interests of older people at all levels of government, plus volunteer legislative committees that are active in every state.
▶ More than 4,000 local chapters with a range of activities and volunteer projects, from teaching to helping out at the polls.
▶ Volunteer-staffed programs such as tax-preparation assistance, driver retraining, widowed-persons counseling, and Medicare assistance.
▶ Special programs in a wide range of subjects, such as

consumer affairs, legal counseling, financial information, housing and health advocacy, women's activities, and crime reduction.

▶ Free publications on a large number of subjects relevant to your life.

▶ And much more.

For information: AARP, 601 E St. NW, Washington, DC 20049; 202-434-AARP.

CANADIAN ASSOCIATION OF RETIRED PERSONS

CARP, a nonprofit association for Canadians over 50, lobbies governments on the issues of concern to the older population, such as medical care, housing, and long-term care. It also offers members group rates for health, property, and travel insurance; a group benefits extension program for people who stop working and leave their health insurance behind; a home equity annuity program; and discounts on hotels, car rentals, theaters, and CARP-sponsored tours and excursions planned by major tour companies. Its informative newspaper is published six times a year and is part of the membership package. Membership costs $10 a year or $25 for three years and includes spouses.

For information: CARP, 27 Queen St., Ste. 1304, Toronto, ON M5C 2M6; 416-363-8748.

CANADIAN SNOWBIRD ASSOCIATION

CSA is an organization formed to represent the interests of Canadian snowbirds, people who flee the winter snow for the sun and palm trees of the U.S. southern states. As their advocate and lobbying group, CSA addresses issues of concern to Canadian seniors such as health care, absentee voting rights, cross border problems, residency requirements, U.S. tax laws for Canadians wintering abroad, and estate tax rules on vacation property in the U.S. owned by Canadians. And it sells travel insurance as well as out-of-country health insurance.

Membership costs $5 a year, and benefits include a bimonthly magazine, group travel offerings, a currency exchange program, mail-order pharmacy services, discounted prescriptions and telephone calls, discounts on Days Inns room rates, and social gatherings in popular snowbird locations such as Florida and Arizona.
For information: Canadian Snowbird Association, 180 Lesmill Rd., North York, ON M3B 2T5; 800-265-3200.

CATHOLIC GOLDEN AGE

A Catholic nonprofit organization that is concerned with issues affecting older citizens, such as health care, housing, and social security benefits, CGA has well over a million members and more than 200 chapters throughout the country. It offers many good things to its members who must be over 50. These include spiritual benefits, such as masses and prayers worldwide, and practical benefits, such as discounts on hotels, campgrounds, car rentals, and prescriptions. Other offerings include group insurance plans, pilgrimage and group travel programs, and an automobile club. Membership costs $8 a year or $19 for three years.
For information: Catholic Golden Age, 430 Penn Ave., Scranton, PA 18503; 800-233-4697.

NATIONAL COUNCIL OF SENIOR CITIZENS

An advocacy organization, NCSC lobbies on the local, state, and national level for legislation benefiting older Americans. With about 5 million members, it has carried on many successful campaigns concerning Medicare, housing, health care, social security, and the like.

Although NCSC's major focus is its legislative program, it also has a local club network, social events, prescription discounts, group rates on supplemental health insurance, automobile insurance, and travel discounts, plus a newspaper that keeps you up to date on all of the above.

For information: National Council of Senior Citizens, 1331 F St. NW, Washington, DC 20004; 202-347-8800.

NATIONAL ASSOCIATION FOR
RETIRED CREDIT UNION PEOPLE

Obviously, not everybody can join this club, but those who do will get some good benefits. These include a magazine called *Prime Times*, a newsletter, car-rental discounts, Medicare supplement insurance, pharmacy discounts, lodging discounts at some hotels and campgrounds, and a motor club. Also, discounted travel packages and tours.

For information: NARCUP, PO Box 391, Madison, WI 53701; 608-232-6070.

NATIONAL ASSOCIATION OF
RETIRED FEDERAL EMPLOYEES

As you have probably gathered, this is an association of federal retirees and families. Its primary mission is to protect the earned benefits of retired federal employees

via its lobbying program in Washington. Members receive a monthly magazine and are entitled to discounts and special services.
For information: NARFE, 1533 New Hampshire Ave. NW, Washington, DC 20036; 202-234-0832.

OLDER WOMEN'S LEAGUE

The league is an advocacy group that works to improve the lot of older women in this country—not an easy job. Through a national organization and local chapters, it provides educational materials, training for citizen advocates, informational publications and the like, dealing with the important issues facing women as they grow older.
For information: Older Women's League, 666 11th St. NW, Ste. 700, Washington, DC 20001; 202-783-6686.

NATIONAL ALLIANCE OF SENIOR CITIZENS

This national lobbying organization with more than two million members has a decidedly conservative tilt-to-the-right bias, so people with middle-of-the-road or liberal views would not feel too much at home here. It works to influence national policy "on key issues of great importance to America and her future." As a member you receive newsletters and benefits that include group insurance, prescription discounts, discounts on car rentals, lodgings, moving expenses, and an automobile club.
For information: National Alliance of Senior Citizens, 1700 18th St. NW, Ste. 401, Washington, DC 20009; 202-986-0117.

GRAY PANTHERS

With thousands of members of all ages, the Gray Panthers speak up for the rights of older Americans, lobbying government, industry, and agencies to consider the needs and wishes of this important block of voters. Major areas of concern are social security, housing, health care, nursing homes, and attitudes.

For information: Gray Panthers, 2025 Pennsylvania Ave. NW, Ste. 821, Washington, DC 20006; 202-466-3132.

THE RETIRED OFFICERS ASSOCIATION

This group is open to anyone who has been a commissioned or warrant officer in the seven U.S. uniformed services. Members receive lobbying representation on Capitol Hill and a magazine with articles devoted to matters of special interest to them. They may also take advantage of several benefits, including discounts on car rentals and motel lodgings, a travel program with "military fares" to many overseas destinations, sports tournaments, a mail-order prescription program, group health and life insurance plans, and a car lease-purchase plan. TROA also has many autonomous local chapters with their own activities and membership fees.

For information: The Retired Officers Association, 201 N. Washington St., Alexandria, VA 22314-2539; 800-245-8762 or 703-549-2311.

Index